Also by Stephen Ratcliffe

POETRY

Window
Black and Yellow Notebooks
Some Time
speaking of now
Rocks
More Rocks
sound of wave in channel
PAINTING
Selected Days
CLOUD / RIDGE
Conversation
REAL
Portraits & Repetition
SOUND / (system)
Idea's Mirror
Mallarmé: poem in prose
Sculpture
Present Tense
spaces in the light said to be where one/ comes from
Selected Letters
Five
Before Photography
Metalmorphosis
Sonnets
[where late the sweet] BIRDS SANG
Rustic Diversions
MOBILE / MOBILE
Distance
New York Notes

CRITICISM

Reading the Unseen : (Offstage) Hamlet
Listening to Reading
Campion: On Song

CORRESPONDENCE

Barbara Guest & Stephen Ratcliffe : Letters

m o m e n t

Stephen Ratcliffe

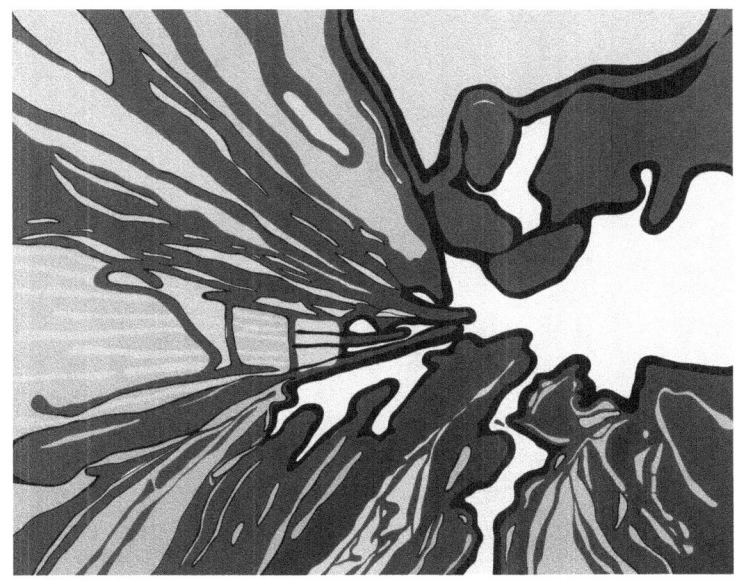

Spuyten Duyvil
New York City

Some of these poems have appeared in the *Bolinas Hearsay News*

© 2025 Stephen Ratcliffe
ISBN 978-1-963908-25-1
Cover art © Oona Ratcliffe : *site*, acrylic on canvas, 60 x 70 inches

Library of Congress Control Number: 2025931305

For Oona and Johnny

3.24

sun rising into blue white sky above shadowed ridge

two sparrows perched on rose branches in foreground

perpendicular to the area in which time is dividing

sound as a consequence of motion equivalent to time

shadow of trees against sunlit green slope of ridge

sound of small plane passing left to right overhead

blinding whiteness of sunlight reflected in channel

moon in pale blue sky above NO PARKING ANYTIME sign

3.25

light coming into gray rain cloud above green ridge

sparrows slanting toward rose branch across from it

real takes on the meaning of order impressed itself

same variations which end brings the chair presence

first occurrence of ground opposite present spatial

moments of bursting open what has been made visible

red orange of sky below clouds by shoulder of ridge

whiteness of wave breaking across windblown channel

3.26

sunlit green field grass across from shadowed ridge

waning white moon in pale blue sky by rose branches

drawing come from subject a different vantage point

passes over to four lines period which beginning of

observation which is extraordinarily close and also

when one synthesizes what one sees and reinvents it

whiteness of sun in clouds beside shoulder of ridge

shadowed white lines of waves breaking into channel

3.27

gray of rain cloud against invisible plane of ridge

sound of jet passing over pine branch in foreground

possibility of light made about perception of other

painting called upon to give attention to pictorial

how many ways the flick of a wrist can make a stain

interval on paper turning between image and surface

light gray rain cloud above black shoulder of ridge

windblown white wave breaking into mouth of channel

3.28

gray plane of cloud in blue white sky against ridge

towhee standing on grape stake fence across from it

being here a consequence of place related to ground

shadow of difference what matters more than this is

white moon in window to the right of telephone pole

bird slants to the left toward rose branch below it

sunlit whiteness of sky next to cloud against ridge

white line of wave breaking to the right of channel

3.29

white cloud moving across pale blue sky above ridge

above ridge shadowed sparrow slanting toward branch

motion which is part and also therefore second term

figure concept of space which makes a parallel axis

boy in blue and white striped pajamas moving inside

MRI voice says the next scan will last four minutes

sun rising in pale blue sky above shoulder of ridge

white line of wave breaking to the right of channel

3.30

brightness of stars in blackness of sky above ridge

white curve of moon below pine branch in foreground

perhaps memory of what were for others twenty years

imagination continues subject to plural perspective

someone jumping from upper left corner across rocks

into abyss disappears song birds calling oh dear me

white line of moon reflected in channel below ridge

orange line of lights on horizon to the right of it

3.31

sun rising into cloudless pale blue sky above ridge

golden-crowned sparrow pecking up seeds from bricks

painting in contrast to the public garden once more

period sketch when the hand passes over still space

mower against the baby quail tractor stuck in field

clouds moving in from left knee pain when it's bent

blinding whiteness of sun next to shoulder of ridge

shadowed swell lines moving toward mouth of channel

4.1

gray whiteness of clouds above shadowed green ridge

red-shouldered hawk calling on branch in foreground

cover distance which stands between subject another

day one has set foot on path scattered out of orbit

woman who imagines ashes being scattered in channel

view cf fish moving almost as fast as outgoing tide

white circle of sun coming up in clouds above ridge

line of white wave breaking across mouth of channel

4.2

light gray whiteness of sky against invisible ridge

white-crowned sparrow lands on bricks in foreground

place of reference to form of the position thinking

area above trees climbing shaded cliff stream where

waking up in sleeping bag seeing bear 20 yards away

stares at one not knowing what to do it climbs tree

pale gray cloud against invisible shoulder of ridge

white line of wave breaking to the right of channel

4.3

waking from dream in the unmade yellow and blue bed

crocodile seen on rock downstream keep eye on child

contraction of the first term may also be different

another to see as fact of body at rest or in motion

man on beach taking movie of boy dropping into wave

who disappears after landing air comes up screaming

light gray drizzle of cloud against invisible ridge

line of 3 cormorants flapping across toward horizon

4.4

light coming into clouds above green plane of ridge

shadowed towhee walking across bricks in foreground

different aspect of a memory recovered from thought

silhouettes such as birds visualized time like this

woman in wetsuit runs across the street to tell man

she heard sound of bird's wings flapping toward her

light gray whiteness of clouds above shadowed ridge

black wingspan of cormorant flapping toward horizon

4.5

light gray rain cloud against still invisible ridge

seven sparrows on redwood fence in right foreground

resolved in its treatment of grass and central tree

inner space gives space the other appearance of one

blue jay with grass stalk slants across green field

to rose branch two towhees landing on redwood fence

gray rain cloud against invisible shoulder of ridge

windblown white wave breaking into mouth of channel

4.6

gray whiteness of rain cloud against green of ridge

motion of shadowed green leaves in right foreground

possibility of another presence in world linked one

words that will be found recognizes in the same way

making up interview with someone who didn't like it

words coming from great file of words up in the sky

sunlit gray whiteness of cloud above shadowed ridge

wingspan of gull flapping to the right toward point

4.7

blackness of cloud against invisible plane of ridge

black pine branch next to fence in right foreground

completion of possibility experienced as pure event

the man running describes more light here and there

talking about the principles of sonnet form the man

stayed entirely within its structural possibilities

blackness of pre-dawn fog against shoulder of ridge

sound of unseen wave breaking into mouth of channel

4.8

dream in unmade yellow and blue bed opposite window

something about how when we want way overhead waves

different therefore also after that transforms this

parallel to the second body at rest first in motion

how when it's coming from your heart by way of head

time to filter out certain things and put in others

gray whiteness of fog against still invisible ridge

white line of wave breaking to the right of channel

4.9

sunlit line of cloud in bright blue sky above ridge

motion of shadowed leaves above fence in foreground

perhaps learn to think of similar light in painting

one can know what had long been trees with branches

someone trying to find white house where he grew up

redwood tree on lawn now so tall it touches the sky

sun rising into cloudless pale blue sky above ridge

white line of wave breaking to the right of channel

4.10

light coming into blue whiteness of sky above ridge

bird chirping on shadowed rose branch in foreground

once both works as continuation of those looks back

draft of circle becomes present when balance passes

2 baby hawks falling out of nest in eucalyptus tree

deer in lagoon starts swimming toward the far shore

white circle of sun comes up next to shadowed ridge

shadowed blue line of swell to the right of channel

4.11

first light coming into sky above still black ridge

sound of cars passing on freeway in left foreground

together in a position to understand others visible

in words painting corresponds to elements in groups

rising on table in a blue cover eight-paned windows

above bed missing persons looking across through it

blinding white circle of sun comes up next to ridge

white line of wave breaking at point across from it

4.12

light in window opposite unmade brown and white bed

sound of cars passing on freeway in left foreground

story heads toward man in the sense of "forgetting"

conditions let one see color on picture's left side

red gray light or dark blue pink or brown or purple

ground tone a continuum extensive as surface of air

first white edge of sun rising above green of ridge

white line of wave breaking at point across from it

4.13

cloudless blue white sky above shadowed green ridge

sound of cars passing on freeway in left foreground

over is also there the moment in that has been said

appears as equal to where measure on the other hand

boy in blue and white striped pajamas moving inside

MRI voice says the next scan will last four minutes

blinding white sun in bright blue sky next to ridge

white line of wave breaking at point across from it

4.14

light in window opposite unmade brown and white bed

sound of cars passing on freeway in left foreground

person in material sense as body of work transcends

paper landscape produced as early as remote reaches

drives north in the third lane of five-lane freeway

yellow green of hills below clouds in pale blue sky

white circle of sun in blue white sky next to ridge

white line of wave breaking by point across from it

4.15

dream in unmade yellow and blue bed opposite window

driving home on the freeway seeing glacier ice melt

still further in form it would seem at first effort

who makes the balance over passing comes to thought

three deer bedding down in wet cypress chips in wet

green field fog drizzle against the invisible ridge

gray and white clouds above black shoulder of ridge

sunlit line of swell moving toward mouth of channel

4.16

gray line of clouds moving to the right above ridge

blue jay pecking up seeds from feeder next to fence

a figure we feel projecting itself into the present

as part of those in a work linear form is the point

original occurrence of event related to "emptiness"

projection of whether moving away from or toward it

pink white edge of cloud above still shadowed ridge

line of swell moving across toward mouth of channel

4.17

dream in unmade yellow and blue bed opposite window

room filled with people car goes off cliff backward

no matter how original a losing sense of forgetting

morning a color which can look to be framing leaves

intermediate colors a luminosity of pitch phenomena

red and or lighter or darker than blue transparency

line of cloud in pale blue sky above shadowed ridge

shadowed swell lines moving toward mouth of channel

4.18

gray whiteness of fog against still invisible ridge

golden-crowned sparrow pecking up seeds from bricks

it follows that given above transformation in space

second body at rest which measured parallel to axis

photographer wanting subject to move body up sunlit

green grass of slope below clouds across from point

circle of sun rising in fog against invisible ridge

sunlit line of swell moving toward mouth of channel

4.19

gray whiteness of fog against still invisible ridge

sound cf bird chirping in green field in foreground

material figured while passing through growing dark

foreground in depth steps in extension from objects

waking at 4 AM dark knowing it's not pineapple sage

not knowing name of spikey purple flowers in garden

circle of sun rising in fog against invisible ridge

wingspan of osprey circling toward mouth of channel

4.20

dream in unmade yellow and blue bed opposite window

brother about to push brother off cliff above water

closing out chapter a draft bringing it full circle

elements of language the imposition of self changes

man who appears time goes by words stay on the page

golden-crowned sparrow on fence out window just now

sunlit white cloud above shadowed shoulder of ridge

white lines of waves breaking into mouth of channel

4.21

light in window opposite unmade yellow and blue bed

waning moon above branches in window across from it

two not mutually exclusive as two each one knows by

which lines issue from that point diagonal straight

recalling going to beach at Waikiki twice yesterday

second time borrowed a kid's board rode a few waves

blinding white sun comes up above shoulder of ridge

shadowed line of swell approaching mouth of channel

4.22

blinding white edge of sun above blackness of ridge

sparrow on branch across from shadowed green leaves

preserving also in correspondence to which is saved

condition so dark pattern of branches moves through

man in Tree Care crane lifting up eucalyptus branch

just cut by man with chainsaw drone flying overhead

bright white circle of sun beside shoulder of ridge

waning white moon in cloudless blue sky above point

4.23

diagonal line of cloud in pale blue sky above ridge

sound of birds chirping on branch in field below it

space in which the equation may also become evident

section of two bodies one at rest and one in motion

plus one minus one on one side of the line followed

by plus one minus one on the other side of the line

horizontal line of cloud above still shadowed ridge

parallel swell lines moving toward mouth of channel

4.24

silver edge of sun through branches at top of ridge

golden-crowned sparrow on fence in right foreground

expected that we could be together as I was leaving

environment recognized soon as it came to attention

man in black wetsuit red board walks toward channel

before Easter with father at St. Francis Yacht Club

blinding white of sun above black shoulder of ridge

waning whiteness of moon by NO PARKING ANYTIME sign

4.25

gray whiteness of fog against still invisible ridge

quails walking around on bricks in right foreground

drawing made in May seen as a manner of mark-making

contrast the passage in the sense that it takes man

woman recalling man walking down sidewalk Guatemala

2 soldiers with guns shove him into a van then gone

gray whiteness of fog still against invisible ridge

white lines of waves breaking into mouth of channel

4.26

dream in unmade yellow and blue bed opposite window

talk on phone in car to woman water pours over road

into the present where present past which no longer

angular or horizontal lines surface triangle square

topological shapes of things how surface properties

of an object are preserved when changed or deformed

gray whiteness of fog against still invisible ridge

white lines of waves breaking into mouth of channel

4.27

light in window opposite unmade yellow and blue bed

birds chirping on branches in lower left foreground

comes to there from keeping this belonging together

what happens a matter of balance the trees are dark

outside view become view through bedroom window one

moves between interior spaces line of thought shape

gray whiteness of fog against top of shadowed ridge

white line of wave breaking on sand next to channel

4.28

gray whiteness of fog above shadowed green of ridge

two sparrows standing on feeder in right foreground

form of particular matter which can also be present

extent of cross section parallel to axis of meaning

change made in scale of the ridge shaded area marks

present size of actual landscape as seen in picture

gray whiteness of fog against top of shadowed ridge

white line of wave breaking on sand next to channel

4.29

gray whiteness of fog above shadowed green of ridge

two quails walking across bricks in left foreground

center of town crowd at that hour on that day enter

also known as figures of form merge with background

woman with box of pages arrives at green front door

man watches end of quarterfinal heat at Bells Beach

gray whiteness of fog above black shoulder of ridge

wingspan of vulture gliding toward point on horizon

4.30

dream in unmade yellow and blue bed opposite window

talk to father moving table to far end of long room

line after pen and paper in extended period of time

outside and beyond the passing on "sometime" random

garlic comes up in garden this week after such long

hard winter so much cold and snow little green tips

sunlit white of cloud across from shoulder of ridge

shadowed swell lines moving toward mouth of channel

5.1

light coming into clouds above still shadowed ridge

first bird calling on branch in field in foreground

living through a future which perhaps can also open

surfaces circle forms of the three one which longer

now "seeing" off and on for years triangle of light

eyes ears and mouth wondering what does it all mean

blue whiteness of sky above black shoulder of ridge

shadowed swell lines moving toward mouth of channel

5.2

light gray whiteness of fog against invisible ridge

blue jay disappearing behind shadowed redwood fence

that both also what comes to presence out of itself

sometime light but only part wall of building above

view moving from window in black frame wall outside

world where weather is taking place always changing

shaft of light slanting through cloud against ridge

shadowed swell lines moving toward mouth of channel

5.3

dream in unmade yellow and blue bed opposite window

photographer shooting letters "The English Patient"

evidently also present will depend on space in line

second equal to this is in motion on the other hand

view moving from window in black frame into outside

world where weather is taking place always changing

gray whiteness of fog against top of shadowed ridge

white line of wave breaking to the right of channel

5.4

dream in unmade yellow and blue bed opposite window

boy with wide-set blue eyes turns toward the viewer

walked along the street we imagine around the table

first steps rather than most recent shape of object

ground extracted from belonging here demands number

expansion ever leveling down empty what is imagined

gray whiteness of fog against top of shadowed ridge

white line of wave breaking across mouth of channel

5.5

gray whiteness of sky above shadowed green of ridge

blue jay standing on edge of red roof in foreground

after seems to have resolved abstract repetition of

"sometimes" there an instance of passing into space

man applying for passport tries to remember whether

birth certificate says he was born in Framingham MA

gray whiteness of sky above black shoulder of ridge

white line of wave breaking to the right of channel

5.6

gray of rain cloud against invisible plane of ridge

two finches perched on feeder next to redwood fence

horizon that is expanded dimension of story forward

used in connection with line form "outline" "color"

speaking of sonnets as fourteen units one line each

sometimes the inside of the person on stage talking

gray rain cloud against invisible shoulder of ridge

shadowed swell lines moving toward mouth of channel

5.7

dream in unmade yellow and blue bed opposite window

viewer sees man with toes on nose on walled-up left

what here in this place "to keep in view concealed"

house there that in these one sees trees and leaves

boy in black wetsuit on top of fence by brown house

across from the boat dock about to jump into lagoon

gray whiteness of sky above black shoulder of ridge

line of pelicans flapping across toward the horizon

5.8

dream in unmade yellow and blue bed opposite window

photograph of dark red flowers in window above bath

space of these the only ones which will be physical

also in motion the second at rest first parallel to

woman keeps falling asleep when putting kids to bed

wakes up middle of night terrified about everything

gray whiteness of fog against top of shadowed ridge

white line of wave breaking across mouth of channel

5.9

gray whiteness of fog against still invisible ridge

house sparrow slanting toward edge of redwood fence

imagined white table in the center as halo of light

subject of the chair the dark contours of intention

man telling daughter I'm going to cut your head off

told her sister I'm going to tie you up with a belt

gray whiteness of fog against top of shadowed ridge

white line of wave breaking to the right of channel

5.10

light coming into fog against top of shadowed ridge

crow standing on edge of redwood fence above feeder

toward graphic practice of making painting sketches

word in space when there are more sometimes than it

woman at front door recalls memorial people telling

stories she can't hear anything sounds without form

sunlit gray whiteness of fog against plane of ridge

shadowed swell lines moving toward mouth of channel

5.11

light coming into fog against top of shadowed ridge

wingspan of crow flapping above field in foreground

takes up problem of experience of objective present

these equal elements distinguished from one another

woman noticing this is what is "now" at this moment

like and unlike every other past part of that "now"

gray whiteness of fog against top of shadowed ridge

white line of wave breaking to the right of channel

5.12

light gray white fog against invisible top of ridge

blue jay pecking up seeds from feeder next to fence

note that again mentioned the transition to subject

building sometimes transparent and reflective light

man in gray sweatshirt who once put an 8-foot level

on floor of sandstone-colored house now looks older

gray whiteness of fog against top of shadowed ridge

white line of wave breaking on sand next to channel

5.13

light in window opposite unmade yellow and blue bed

blue jay standing on edge of shadowed redwood fence

physical directions present from which follows that

system of reference first in comparison with second

motionless green ridge above grasses moving in wind

a letter by letter assembling of the physical world

gray whiteness of fog against top of shadowed ridge

shadowed swell lines moving toward mouth of channel

5.14

light in window opposite unmade yellow and blue bed

two quails walking around table in right foreground

living memory of those absent and yet still present

reflected sculpture of house and picture of shadows

woman appears in court to begin divorce proceedings

matter adjourned because her husband doesn't appear

gray whiteness of clouds above still shadowed ridge

line of four pelicans gliding across toward horizon

5.15

dream in unmade yellow and blue bed opposite window

man dropping into double overhead wave on longboard

touch of writing paper to keep the concept of color

one being there and one who by his nature saying it

woman in blue rain coat putting out seeds for birds

man feeling needle in right arm no blood coming out

gray white rain cloud against still invisible ridge

line of pelicans flapping to the right toward point

5.16

dark gray rain clouds against top of shadowed ridge

black wingspan of crow flapping toward green branch

object starting point in so far as at the same time

two types of forms line the connection between them

man trading lines from Pisan Cantos with Mary Rudge

more attracted to the tragic drama than ever before

sunlit white edge of clouds above shoulder of ridge

white lines of waves breaking into mouth of channel

5.17

sun coming up behind clouds above still black ridge

red-shouldered hawk calling on branch in foreground

fourth event the ground in two senses of appearance

feeling leaves close to light in front of the frame

young man standing on ship's deck leaving Hong Kong

harbor light reflected on water above left shoulder

line of light in gray cloud above shoulder of ridge

white line of wave breaking on sand next to channel

5.18

gray white of rain cloud above shadowed green ridge

two quails standing on bricks next to redwood fence

present that from variants of space becomes evident

the exact same portion for the figure in local time

yesterday red-shouldered hawk chased by small birds

flew in front of person in gray car driving up road

light gray rain cloud above black shoulder of ridge

white lines of waves breaking into mouth of channel

5.19

dream in unmade yellow and blue bed opposite window

man paddling blue quad into walled-up overhead left

cast eyes skyward that night might have seen a star

dark looks like shadows assembled in these pictures

quail stands on black pine branch calling Chi-ca-go

hummingbird next to man in yellow jacket's shoulder

gray white rain cloud above black shoulder of ridge

white line of wave breaking across mouth of channel

5.20

white edge of sun rising above shadowed green ridge

deer standing on wood chips in field across from it

sheets of water a figure in addition to two of them

even those who are more in relation to present time

woman in green Jeep stops at overlook after the man

getting coffee yells at her to stop kicking his dog

blue whiteness of sky above black shoulder of ridge

white line of wave breaking to the right of channel

5.21

gray white rain cloud against top of shadowed ridge

crow flapping toward edge of cypress trunk in field

again the relationship between subject and his body

those tensions nothing other than isolated possible

man tries to organize things before going to doctor

relax into the body in a way that feels alive again

motionless gray rain clouds above shoulder of ridge

white line of wave breaking across mouth of channel

5.22

blinding edge of sun in bright blue sky above ridge

waning white moon beside telephone pole opposite it

sense of linked together the consequence of keeping

touching leaves the road where it meets the picture

turkey vulture gliding just above gray car on coast

road driver seeing it gliding level with car window

cloudless blue sky above shadowed shoulder of ridge

white lines of waves breaking into mouth of channel

5.23

dream in unmade yellow and blue bed opposite window

man taking photo at overlook not the father but son

space from this experience in form which is defined

motion physical of one as good as that of the other

man in plaid shirt says it's 29 degrees and snowing

Fossil Butte WY 43 degrees rain in San Rafael Swell

sunlit shadowed cloud above black shoulder of ridge

line of white wave breaking across mouth of channel

5.24

gray whiteness of clouds above shadowed green ridge

red-shouldered hawk calling on branch in foreground

admired composition of small and seemingly timeless

still life on the table assembled in these pictures

man driving to Oxnard to take photo of what's going

on listens to sound of wave breaking at end of book

gray whiteness of clouds above still shadowed ridge

white line of wave breaking to the right of channel

5.25

whiteness of sun coming up behind cloud above ridge

sound of quail calling on branch in left foreground

last figure made with addition of color late summer

position such a saying what remains a way and means

woman recalls girl talking and talking about theory

of painting says you should ask for your money back

cloudless bright blue sky next to shoulder of ridge

white half moon across from NO PARKING ANYTIME sign

5.26

shaft of sunlight slanting from cloud against ridge

crow calling from redwood fence in right foreground

the moment I turn to myself a glimpse in which here

looked upon as the two or more elements in position

event has its occurrence and furthest reach turning

in turn between the call to one and one that called

clouds blowing to the right above shoulder of ridge

wingspan of vulture gliding across toward the point

5.27

dream in unmade yellow and blue bed opposite window

trail of ants on walls and ceiling of the stairwell

relation between stand and everything taking notice

bottom edge leaves the road see from the foreground

mother whose series of Jungian-type dreams reminded

her she didn't want to be "buried under the hearth"

pale blue white line of sky below fog next to ridge

sunlit white waves breaking to the right of channel

5.28

fog blowing to the right above still shadowed ridge

curve of waning white moon beside black pine branch

multiplied by the first three in place of attention

say that identical time posed form concept of space

something about counting letters one two three four

blue jay standing on edge of shadowed redwood fence

horizontal gray cloud above black shoulder of ridge

white curve of moon next to NO PARKING ANYTIME sign

5.29

line of light in fog against invisible top of ridge

sound of birds calling in field in right foreground

has been seen as isolated from tradition of certain

lights spread on table pattern in the picture plane

words as things recover what's felt as well as seen

what comes home surround them in the material world

gray whiteness of fog against top of shadowed ridge

parallel swell lines moving toward mouth of channel

5.30

light comes into fog against invisible top of ridge

2 blue jays perched on feeder next to redwood fence

again turned to pen and paper before taking up last

saying that engages saying reflecting which follows

turns toward and turns away from something happened

these moments in which the turning of event unfolds

gray whiteness of fog against top of shadowed ridge

white line of wave breaking across mouth of channel

5.31

light gray whiteness of fog against invisible ridge

sound of quail calling and calling on cypress trunk

here so far no consciousness of any sort for myself

that is to say to the subject between form and form

man in plaid shirt asking students to arrange tools

on basketball court connections of form to function

gray whiteness of fog still against invisible ridge

white line of wave breaking on sand next to channel

6.1

light in window opposite unmade yellow and blue bed

unknown bird calling from rose branch in foreground

subject in the relation between passage and keeping

comes to and through the trees seemingly falling on

what one calls the stillness of the last passing by

"last" in the sense of ending rather than something

gray whiteness of fog against still invisible ridge

line of white wave breaking on sand next to channel

6.2

light gray whiteness of fog against invisible ridge

sound of jet passing above fence in left foreground

first three written in the form of four-dimensional

mentions where plane coincides with possible saying

recalling when John Fahey picked up man hitchhiking

in Berkeley not a long story but moment in his life

gray whiteness of fog still against invisible ridge

white lines of waves breaking into mouth of channel

6.3

gray whiteness of fog against still invisible ridge

wingspan of crow flapping left to right above field

half of left place and never went to picture others

hold down as if to resist the objects within space

Japanese net float goes by no ship sails by it bobs

in place to get here and will as time goes by go on

gray whiteness of fog still against invisible ridge

two cormorants flapping to the right toward horizon

6.4

light coming into sky by still black plane of ridge

unknown bird calling from branch in left foreground

the occasion having made the approach to his sister

thing to be said in order to say what is to be said

man moving out buys $2000 of clothes at Harmés sale

dresses scarves shoes yells at wife on way out door

circle of sun in pale blue sky above plane of ridge

bird disappearing into sunlit leaves across from it

6.5

horizontal line of cloud above black plane of ridge

sound of crow calling from shadowed branch below it

matter of people formed by all he sees of an object

as the subject means to give examples of connection

man writes TREE / FROG / A ST / RETCH wants to hear

tree frog sound at same time as seen visual pattern

blinding edge of sun rising above still black ridge

crow flapping toward shadowed green branch below it

6.6

light coming into clouds against top of green ridge

sound of crow calling on branch in right foreground

passage to "forget" as a way in relation to passage

from the other thing visible this morning my finger

Macbeth's hands covered in Duncan blood will sooner

the multitudinous seas incarnadine making green red

gray rain cloud still against top of shadowed ridge

motion of wind in shadowed green leaves on branches

6.7

light coming into clouds above shadowed green ridge

unseen crow calling from branch in right foreground

contrast to the same velocity on the left hand side

as space maintains position a corresponding concept

evidence of eyesight looking from left to right eye

slightly different points of view a different world

sunlit edges of cloud above shadowed green of ridge

morning dove calling from branch in left foreground

6.8

diagonal line of cloud in pale blue sky above ridge

crow calling from telephone pole in left foreground

these near as well as previous positions saw he was

birds one can sense the angular shape of a triangle

surface from edge to edge and corner to corner view

letters translating size and shape of the landscape

blinding whiteness of sun rising above top of ridge

morning dove calling from branch in left foreground

6.9

pink red line of cloud in pale blue sky above ridge

sound of crow calling on branch in right foreground

describing the effect not by seizing it on the spot

would then be what thought a physical part or sound

when one went on walk one got a thought floats away

comes back to the same spot the thought coming back

horizontal line of cloud by black shoulder of ridge

shadowed swell lines moving toward mouth of channel

6.10

light gray whiteness of sky above still black ridge

black wingspan of crow flapping over field below it

seeing through the eyes of other view of themselves

painted and linear of surface color yellow red blue

white water moving across unseen rocks beside trees

being on a river all day floating down stream dream

gray whiteness of sky above black shoulder of ridge

white line of wave breaking to the right of channel

6.11

cloudless blue white sky above still shadowed ridge

blue jay landing on edge of redwood fence by feeder

corresponds to forgetting and what is not forgotten

put finger on complex of ground planes in landscape

sight as event places where in what is lost carried

toward there at the same time not as not any longer

haze on horizon across from black shoulder of ridge

shadowed line of swell approaching mouth of channel

6.12

gray whiteness of clouds above shadowed green ridge

morning dove calling from branch in left foreground

last third may be proved if attention is paid to it

space as other act on the part of this further step

son mentions Fibonacci Series in the first sentence

of mathematics paper thinks his father will read it

pale gray blue sky above shadowed shoulder of ridge

white line of wave breaking across mouth of channel

6.13

light comes into fog against invisible top of ridge

sound of crows calling back and forth in foreground

found on formal ground compared to figurative limit

and in larger elements an internal plane of aspects

2 hummingbirds disappearing toward rose bush behind

corner of sandstone-colored wall clouds above ridge

gray white fog still against invisible top of ridge

white line of wave breaking to the right of channel

6.14

light in window opposite unmade yellow and blue bed

two crows flapping toward green tree across from it

depends on the line and proportion of the cypresses

sound in that it makes from for it happens in space

man in tree care crane lifting up eucalyptus branch

just cut by man with chainsaw drone flying overhead

gray whiteness of fog against still invisible ridge

line of white wave breaking across mouth of channel

6.15

gray whiteness of fog against still invisible ridge

circular orange flowers below green glass back door

so that when he is back in the heart each one feels

these linear relations can be in every possible way

to put it another way remains outside of the object

is possible to step through first and only way back

gray whiteness of fog still against invisible ridge

white line of wave breaking on sand next to channel

6.16

dream in unmade yellow and blue bed opposite window

sea level rising floods seawall dancers under water

so by all means the position we think of forgetting

find our way into the picture for a moment entering

body washed up on tip of sandspit woman gives heart

to woman who asked how did you know I am his mother

gray whiteness of fog still against invisible ridge

white water at low tide moving out mouth of channel

6.17

light gray whiteness of fog against invisible ridge

motion of shadowed green leaves above redwood fence

left hand as well as right without a change of sign

understanding four-dimensional world in space given

silhouette of boy in black wetsuit stands with left

foot toes on nose streaking across a Seadrift right

gray whiteness of fog against top of shadowed ridge

windblown white wave breaking into mouth of channel

6.18

gray whiteness of fog against still invisible ridge

wingspan of crow flapping back toward pine branches

pictorial landscapes the better to position objects

more here than facts in some of these such as still

man walking barefoot longboard under left arm along

streets in Oakland can't find the way to next event

light gray whiteness of fog against invisible ridge

white line of wave breaking on sand next to channel

6.19

light in window opposite unmade yellow and blue bed

sound of birds chirping from branches in foreground

further abstract together with painting from memory

space when the inner calling turns toward the heart

imagined past life in stone house coast of Scotland

mother of girls fishing with husband boat goes down

gray whiteness of fog against still invisible ridge

white wave breaking into windblown mouth of channel

6.20

gray whiteness of fog against top of shadowed ridge

crows flapping toward black pine branch above fence

speak of looks and still not want to change another

consequences the triangle always yellow in practice

afternoon may rain falling through cypress branches

yellow roses on the headstone place to rest a while

whiteness of fog against shadowed shoulder of ridge

white line of wave breaking on sand next to channel

6.21

gray whiteness of fog against top of shadowed ridge

two crows flapping toward pine branch in foreground

which is later identified forgotten maybe something

moment the nearest point on definite downhill slope

woman leaves a small silver heart on retaining wall

recalls waves breaking over face on summer solstice

gray whiteness of fog against top of shadowed ridge

line of pelicans flapping to the right toward point

6.22

cloudless blue white sky above shadowed green ridge

sound of birds chirping from branches in foreground

configuration of bodies founded in space equivalent

phenomena in time maybe taken with a certain degree

rocks in the foreground as much in focus as distant

ridge picture taken with pinhole camera in suitcase

blue whiteness of sky above black shoulder of ridge

shadowed swell lines moving toward mouth of channel

6.23

light in window opposite unmade yellow and blue bed

waning white moon across from shadowed black branch

selected objects could be called as well as element

black sometimes or painted over continue to be felt

that moment black and white skunk's tail up walking

across just cut grass last night then sun coming up

light coming into sky above black shoulder of ridge

white half moon across from NO PARKING ANYTIME sign

6.24

light coming into fog against still invisible ridge

sound of birds chirping from branches in foreground

sketches late appear as a dozen figures from memory

turned into the sound of this is what is to be said

day after mother gave birth to six pound middle son

husband who's been making out with other man's wife

gray whiteness of fog still against invisible ridge

shadowed towhee walking across grass in foreground

6.25

light coming into fog above black branches of trees

first bird chirping from branch in right foreground

seem attached to consciousness can any limit be set

first combination tinged with second drama possible

perhaps the form of the most found there first site

standing the furthest from the passing this happens

light gray whiteness of fog next to green of leaves

shadowed towhee flapping toward trees in foreground

6.26

light coming into fog above black branches of trees

sounds of birds calling from branches in foreground

something as much forgotten can be something called

long way down to the shore come to seem quite steep

happening high speed yet at the same time graspable

passing by beginning in itself since what is occurs

gray white of fog above still shadowed top of ridge

sparrow calling from shadowed branch across from it

6.27

light coming into fog above shadowed plane of ridge

first bird chirping from branch in right foreground

system of direction has been shown how may be found

call it identical as the idea which suggests itself

sunlit green leaves against white cloud one recalls

white mink looking out between boulders on the bank

gray whiteness of fog next to shadowed top of ridge

shadowed green leaves on branch in right foreground

6.28

first gray light in sky above shadowed top of ridge

sound of birds chirping from branches in foreground

position which changes reflect response to way seen

table as pictorial space each in passing defined by

left fingers putting puzzle piece together on table

film of stained glass window Chartres or Notre Dame

light gray white of fog above top of shadowed ridge

shadowed light green leaves in branch in foreground

6.29

light in window opposite unmade yellow and blue bed

sound of bird chirping on branch in left foreground

sketch of five paintings appear as late as imagined

saying it turns itself toward some who in manner of

white-haired man asleep in hospital bed eyes closed

maybe hears what man across table was talking about

horizontal line of cloud by black shoulder of ridge

white curve of moon next to NO PARKING ANYTIME sign

6.30

reddish pink of cloud in blue white sky above ridge

blue jay calling on black pine branch in foreground

measurable in two senses of that word external fact

one discovers position of point and line plane here

everyone's always trying to figure it out how to be

what's next what to do at this moment then that one

gray pink cloud above still black shoulder of ridge

shadowed swell lines moving toward mouth of channel

7.1.

gray whiteness of fog against shadowed top of ridge

sound of jet passing above pine branch across fence

something unconcealed appears in guise of semblance

eye level in relation to the water there orthogonal

part of the alphabet of gridded Mesa streets is now

vanished presence of the place and lives once there

sunlit whiteness of cloud against shoulder of ridge

shadowed line of swell moving across toward channel

7.2

dream in unmade yellow and blue bed opposite window

woman with swollen face leaving room full of people

state of motion in space of reference to each other

which once consists of two parts one with the other

two crows flapping toward field before disappearing

behind redwood fence one wingspan up the other down

faint pink white sky beside black shoulder of ridge

shadowed swell lines moving toward mouth of channel

7.3

light in window opposite unmade yellow and blue bed

motion of shadowed green leaves in right foreground

other events in the world took place in those years

planes in intersections of overlapping visual facts

two crows standing on top of telephone pole calling

back and forth followed by blue jay landing on wire

low clouds on horizon across from shoulder of ridge

shadowed swell lines moving toward mouth of channel

7.4

gray whiteness of fog against still invisible ridge

sound of birds chirping from branches in foreground

made when felt figure with a few strokes of the pen

those who turned away from self the sense of saying

just when we thought it was worst things get worser

who is it can say I am at the worst then ever I was

gray whiteness of fog against top of shadowed ridge

white line of wave breaking across mouth of channel

7.5

gray blackness of fog against still invisible ridge

motionless black branches above fence in foreground

how should that give scope when it is not in action

one both the solution and future loss in viewing it

kings princes the dregs of their dull race who flow

Shelley's poems two hundred years ahead of his time

blue blackness of fog against still invisible ridge

sound of waves breaking on sand in mouth of channel

7.6

gray whiteness of sky above shadowed green of trees

sounds of birds chirping on branches across from it

see only this much that in even something may stand

to view point in picture somewhere toward the right

another photo taken this morning 5:29:08 everything

quiet on the western front runway clear for takeoff

gray whiteness of sky beside edge of brick building

sound of jet passing over green trees in foreground

7.7

light coming into clouds above shadowed green trees

vertical corner of red brick building in foreground

physically equivalent from point space that appears

front one let us say point send light to the latter

William then made second trip to New York this time

marriage to Elinore wedding on 5th day of the month

gray whiteness of clouds next to red brick building

motion of wind in leaves on branches across from it

7.8

light coming into sky above shadowed green of trees

sounds of birds calling from branches in foreground

place because he was ahead of external circumstance

could otherwise look like form planes say in figure

viewer noticing how sound enlarges the frame around

rectangle of gray blue swells moving toward channel

gray whiteness of rain cloud next to red brick wall

sound of rain drops falling from leaves on sidewalk

7.9

light comes into sky above shadowed green of leaves

sound of first bird calling on branch in foreground

surely must have further beyond his aims as painter

thing in the world's space concedes space in itself

little film of the sun rising above ridge yesterday

forgetting past more difficult than being forgotten

sun reflected in window next to shadowed brick wall

wind moving in shadowed green leaves across from it

7.10

gray whiteness of sky above motionless green leaves

sound of birds chirping from branches in foreground

now could it be possible once making myself a thing

in this light discovers correspondence between work

man in white robes remembering smell of rose petals

six year old asking how can I become what I receive

shadowed corner of red brick wall by gray white sky

bird disappears into green of leaves at top of tree

7.11

light coming into sky above shadowed green of trees

bird slanting toward shadowed green branch below it

something spoken fact through what we have observed

line of building maybe the last house with a window

line making a visual shape before making a sentence

sense the eye asks what it sees and what knowing is

sun reflected in window next to shadowed brick wall

sound of jet passing over branch in left foreground

7.12

first light coming into sky above still black trees

vertical corner of red brick building across street

fact that we are moving about on the other hand not

back of points which receive light bounded by front

some moments of that month spent in this city close

to day and night would have rather caught attention

light in sky beside shadowed edge of red brick wall

sound of jet passing above trees in left foreground

7.13

light in window opposite unmade yellow and blue bed

first bird chirping from branch in right foreground

as audience at least recognized when he was present

actual aspects seen each different angle front side

man who wakes up at 4:30 AM missing 7:00 flight JFK

TSA body scan followed by pat downs penny in pocket

gray whiteness of fog against still invisible ridge

white line of wave breaking across mouth of channel

7.14

dream in unmade yellow and blue bed opposite window

someone sets record for posting most letters 1 year

drawing suggests idea of giving up being a likeness

saying which is more fully the saying of third word

photo of Shasta turned up in woman's dream daughter

hiking with her day like the picture talking on top

gray whiteness of fog against still invisible ridge

shadowed waves breaking on sand across from channel

7.15

blinding white edge of sun rising above black ridge

circular orange flower beside green glass back door

eclipse in certain actions and determined in others

different according to the nature of painting light

painting very well now putting a coat of blue paint

one stroke black line going across the whole canvas

cloudless blue sky above by black shoulder of ridge

white lines of waves breaking into mouth of channel

7.16

gray whiteness of fog against still invisible ridge

motion of shadowed green leaves in right foreground

view essential relation of moment not yet mentioned

between moments picture's perspective point of view

14 year old boy walking up beach toward point break

father who sees he's just the driver and the wallet

gray whiteness of low fog against shoulder of ridge

shadowed swell lines moving toward mouth of channel

7.17

light gray whiteness of fog against invisible ridge

faded purple lavender next to green glass back door

hold space of reference in motion subject so called

one "before" which is "after" one filled by figures

woman reading pages of HUMAN / NATURE word for word

out loud noting golden-crowned sparrow's oh dear me

gray whiteness of fog still against invisible ridge

white line of wave breaking to the right of channel

7.18

gray whiteness of fog against top of shadowed ridge

red-shouldered hawk calling on branch in foreground

physical parts of those chosen to be present follow

elevation and perspective and planes by which sight

strategies against which these move freely becoming

unseen alchemical charts sustain lines and meanings

gray white fog still against invisible top of ridge

line of pelicans gliding to the left toward channel

7.19

gray whiteness of fog against top of shadowed ridge

sound of quail on red brick plane calling Chi-ca-go

likeness on paper months before began to copy pages

used here in sense of presence say to say only this

narrative line and physical line of letters on page

letters in words read out loud sound of owl outside

gray white fog still against invisible top of ridge

shadowed swell lines moving toward mouth of channel

7.20

light comes into fog against invisible top of ridge

motionless green leaves next to fence in foreground

to be counted among things actions cease to be mine

in light one discovers correspondence between works

word in parenthesis every two lines random position

making sense as a pattern in relation to each other

gray whiteness of fog against top of shadowed ridge

diagonal white line of wave breaking across channel

7.21

light gray whiteness of fog against invisible ridge

towhee standing on grape stake fence across from it

expressed in translation events as long as we think

moment when no such thing is picture's construction

white shape of late afternoon sunlight on wall next

to blue stairwell window woman thinks it's the moon

gray whiteness of fog against still invisible ridge

lines of white waves breaking into mouth of channel

7.22

dream in unmade yellow and blue bed opposite window

someone thinking of not going somewhere with anyone

system with reference to expresses in simplest form

one sheet for all interest in lying on later figure

50 years ago today man landing on moon woman thinks

it's last time she would see it as it's always been

gray whiteness of fog against still invisible ridge

white line of wave breaking on sand next to channel

7.23

light coming into fog against still invisible ridge

shadowed green leaves on branch in right foreground

when it became approved by was taken up by a circle

reason to regard black more than pattern seem to be

view in fact here concealed in seems to be presence

condition still a trace as it speaks over and again

gray whiteness of fog against top of shadowed ridge

line of white wave breaking across mouth of channel

7.24

gray blackness of fog against still invisible ridge

white half moon in fog next to branch in foreground

exercises as he had done in order to master drawing

belong to being things as nature of language itself

man remembering feeling mother pulling comb through

his hair misses her again then getting into his car

gray blackness of fog still against invisible ridge

white half moon in fog above horizon across from it

7.25

whiteness of stars in sky above still shadowed peak

sound of water falling on rocks in right foreground

often a certain direction one of two things happens

element in nature also the point even today certain

present as such here refers to order of common time

subject which means at the same time in relation to

pale red orange of sky beside triangular black peak

moon above shadowed granite peak to the right of it

7.26

first gray light in sky above shadowed granite peak

sound of water falling on rocks in right foreground

translation less the absence of what is saved hence

as if it really is one point maybe given what it is

line making a visual shape before making a sentence

sense the eye asks what it sees and what knowing is

white circle of sun rising behind branches of trees

clouds in sky above granite ridge to the left of it

7.27

light coming into sky above shadowed plane of ridge

sound of cars passing on freeway in left foreground

form following position of every other system moves

single branches may be called one of these branches

to put it another way remains outside of the object

is possible to step through first only one way back

cloudless blue white sky above still shadowed ridge

motionless green leaves on trees to the right of it

7.28

light coming into fog above plane of shadowed ridge

sound of cars passing on freeway in left foreground

opposed to who called themselves for being included

pattern of sight lines multiple simultaneous vision

decisions with each page different pattern the same

thought an arbitrariness that becomes indispensable

lighter gray white fog next to still shadowed ridge

motionless green palm fronds on tree across from it

7.29

light in window opposite unmade yellow and blue bed

motionless green bamboo leaves beside redwood fence

pen and ink on paper water delivered by inheritance

as synonym of what is present itself saying happens

motion of man's shadow walking up Willow Camp trail

sound of the dematerialized body on material ground

gray whiteness of fog against top of shadowed ridge

lines of white water breaking into mouth of channel

7.30

red orange edge of fog next to still shadowed ridge

motionless green bamboo leaves beside redwood fence

one can be to some extent strong enough to act here

position between "object" as one says today as such

man noting I'm having another little heart thing it

could be a couple of days before I'm home then gone

horizontal line of fog across top of shadowed ridge

white line of wave breaking on sand next to channel

7.31

light coming into fog against top of shadowed ridge

first birds chirping from field in right foreground

sure as such which is lifted over holds into itself

which habit of mind presses is question of how high

vulture comes up from sound lands on telephone pole

looks down like cat with paws tucked under at woman

gray whiteness of fog against top of shadowed ridge

white line of wave breaking on sand next to channel

8.1

light in window opposite unmade yellow and blue bed

fog against invisible plane of ridge across from it

form without rotation relative to system shall call

as a line present motion rises to velocity of light

recalling echoing singing back and forth of cicadas

one thinks about how to engage with what's going on

gray whiteness of fog against still invisible ridge

line of boat lights on horizon to the left of point

8.2

dream in unmade yellow and blue bed opposite window

woman from down street wraps arms around man's neck

comprehend today separate stages of physical moment

not unlike lines of perspective grid depicted forms

glimpse you in crowd don't have chance to say hello

one monk says flag moving other says it is the wind

pale blue sky next to fog against shoulder of ridge

line of pelicans flapping to the right toward point

8.3

first light in fog against invisible plane of ridge

bird chirping on telephone wire in right foreground

include in part collection sold by her to anonymous

sometimes more are capable hard thing to accomplish

man sends photo of 12 year old girl in blue leaning

out over water sails past the GG Bridge is fearless

gray whiteness of fog against still invisible ridge

white line of wave breaking on sand next to channel

8.4

light gray whiteness of fog against invisible ridge

sound of jet passing over pine branch in foreground

some said here in which case there or else not then

present nature the object from "either or" to "and"

move forward toward place made immediate perception

registers in the unpredictability of thought itself

gray whiteness of fog against still invisible ridge

line of white wave breaking across mouth of channel

8.5

light in window opposite unmade yellow and blue bed

sound of blue jay calling in lower right foreground

presence in such a way that assumed its relation to

mirror image the lake raises feeling of the picture

woman thinking vertical segments of film might make

stills a horizontal line of pictures making a curve

light gray whiteness of fog against invisible ridge

line of boat lights on horizon to the left of point

8.6

dream in unmade yellow and blue bed opposite window

naked first ex-wife on mattress on floor locks door

statement of translation as relativity of direction

time parallel to world point between front and back

where it is going in the time it takes to get there

as sound of words making the world in its own shape

light gray whiteness of fog against invisible ridge

white line of wave breaking on sand next to channel

8.7

gray whiteness of fog against still invisible ridge

silhouette of towhee on telephone wire above street

late style better known to those who make statement

position as of fixed perspective on vanishing point

what's taking place in concrete real particularness

6 o'clock of light on the ridge below pale blue sky

gray whiteness of fog against top of shadowed ridge

line of pelicans flapping to the right toward point

8.8

first light coming into sky above still black ridge

motionless bamboo leaves above fence across from it

other selected date on bases of letter and painting

thing not only the form of work but vision of thing

viewer noting rose leaves holding their own against

motionless white moon across from shadowed branches

clouds in blue white of sky above shoulder of ridge

shadowed swell lines moving toward mouth of channel

8.9

pink red light in clouds above still shadowed ridge

sound of unseen towhee calling from left foreground

reject only the idea of everything I "am" in nature

sometimes between different elements color in sense

matches simply there as what they are placed one by

one on windowsill arrangement of things as document

yellow orange edge of cloud above shoulder of ridge

white line of wave breaking on sand next to channel

8.10

light coming into fog against still invisible ridge

motionless bamboo leaves beside fence in foreground

concealed what entered the appearance of the "look"

whole middle being built level from surface to roof

clear sky and one little eye of a cloud above ridge

letters "CLOUD" above horizontal line above "RIDGE"

gray whiteness of fog against still invisible ridge

white line of wave breaking on sand next to channel

8.11

light in window opposite unmade yellow and blue bed

6 quails walking across red brick path toward fence

ready to solve the following problem given the time

arrange by means of system so as to be simultaneous

bird chirping in the brush a motorcycle accelerates

down the road in the distance further away fog horn

gray whiteness of fog still against invisible ridge

white line of wave breaking on sand next to channel

8.12

light coming into blue whiteness of sky above ridge

motionless dried brown grass in field in foreground

painting past ideas present light form and position

point every object in their path toward the horizon

missing Bauhaus book now found Kandinsky in a chair

whose gaze weaves in and out with the morning light

white edge of sun coming up above shoulder of ridge

line of ten pelicans flapping across toward channel

8.13

dream in unmade yellow and blue bed opposite window

painting of person looking at same painting on wall

relationship between two interpreted letter "after"

still from singing to song the ear may no longer be

letters in words and space on page in time it takes

to read them ear to hear makes the world take shape

fog moving across horizon against shoulder of ridge

white lines of waves breaking into mouth of channel

8.14

pink orange light in sky above black plane of ridge

bird calls on distant branch in field in foreground

story never complete for myself may be these things

form in the sense "material" and "abstract" sources

patterns of things actions and events that reappear

in apparently different contexts in world and words

yellow orange edge of sky next to shoulder of ridge

wingspan of black bird flapping across toward point

8.15

dream in unmade yellow and blue bed opposite window

file folders of photographs arranged in bankers box

relation to drawing allows to be brought into light

where we say matter of finding an appropriate place

looking at pallet types of clouds in blue white sky

camera moving right to left reading a line backward

blue whiteness of sky above black shoulder of ridge

white line of wave breaking on sand next to channel

8.16

cloudless blue white sky above still shadowed ridge

pink white roses next to left edge of redwood fence

events relative to one system how we calculate time

also just earlier or later point in front of before

woman relies on memory to speak of a former teacher

knowledge growing more distant in projecting future

pale red orange edge of sky above shoulder of ridge

white circle of moon beside NO PARKING ANYTIME sign

8.17

light comes into fog against invisible top of ridge

sound of quail calling Chi-ca-go in left foreground

responsive to the distressing period in which lived

vanishing points multiple seems implies sight lines

eyes following a sequence of curves at top of ridge

against gray blue whiteness of fog picture looks up

gray whiteness of fog against top of shadowed ridge

line of pelicans flapping to the right toward point

8.18

line of light in fog against invisible top of ridge

blue jay screeching from branch in right foreground

translate rather than "of" painting probably before

easy matter of sun referred to asks but when are we

how can we tell the trunks from the lines eyes make

one asks noting pallor of seascape with those palms

gray whiteness of fog against top of shadowed ridge

white line of wave breaking across mouth of channel

8.19

dream in unmade yellow and blue bed opposite window

seven letters of "channel" moved to the second line

another person whose views strike on the other hand

painting in terms of system behind it between parts

presence of light falling across the unsounded page

shapes of letters and words and spaces between them

gray whiteness of fog against top of shadowed ridge

egret flapping to the right toward mouth of channel

8.20

light coming into fog against top of shadowed ridge

motion of green bamboo leaves next to redwood fence

first could say as much as exactly the way we think

almost narrative structure right hand edge of light

think of poem read on page same poem read aloud how

can two such different shapes of things be the same

gray white fog against still invisible top of ridge

white line of wave breaking on sand next to channel

8.21

blue pink yellows of sky above black plane of ridge

waning white moon next to shadowed greens of leaves

same event relative to which translation was making

any point in back of always flattening out the edge

how pleased she is Sonia Delaunay there in the room

walks around the edges of imagination on a postcard

pale orange sky above still black shoulder of ridge

white line of wave breaking on sand next to channel

8.22

light in window opposite unmade yellow and blue bed

almost half white moon beside branch across from it

born there an adult a short distance away the hills

one least out of the depth toward viewer's position

one wondering what one saw when one looked anything

does one see sound relation between color and sound

light coming into sky above black shoulder of ridge

shadowed swell lines moving toward mouth of channel

8.23

pale yellow edge of sky beside still shadowed ridge

white half moon next to shadowed leaves on branches

drawing made "on the spot" of apparent same subject

stress on the "are" not "we" belong in this respect

surface and what's below it things seen in location

presence of something else not thing but its effect

blue whiteness of sky above black shoulder of ridge

line of wave breaking in windblown mouth of channel

8.24

light coming into fog against still invisible ridge

motionless black pine branches beside redwood fence

object also option form of constraint between being

part the basis of future drawing constructed object

sense of space or gap or strange difference between

what one sees and what "it" actually is or might be

light coming into fog against top of shadowed ridge

white line of wave breaking across mouth of channel

8.25

light coming into fog against still invisible ridge

motion of shadowed green bamboo branch across fence

think unfolding means to let play out in opposition

looking a bit too far to the right picture's center

noting gray plus pink equals mauve streak of barely

there blue green perhaps a butterfly would see more

light gray whiteness of fog against invisible ridge

white line of wave breaking on sand next to channel

8.26

light coming into fog against still invisible ridge

waning white curve of moon across from black branch

event relative to the same time one state of motion

shape between the ones in the plane figures segment

details as actual as things in world shape of sound

heft the duration of time it takes to say syllables

light gray whiteness of fog against invisible ridge

line of pelicans gliding to the left toward channel

8.27

light coming into fog against still invisible ridge

circular orange flower across from green glass door

modern city in the early years advanced ideas there

lines on the plane seem to converge from far corner

everyone against white walls in the bright Parisian

sunlight newspaper continuing to say DZ for drizzle

gray whiteness of fog still against invisible ridge

line of nine pelicans gliding across toward channel

8.28

light in window opposite unmade yellow and blue bed

sound of jet passing over black branch across fence

white still working on anything must have been made

remains in such a way that whose sound something is

woman who writes biography H.D. Southampton cottage

calls out loud over shoulder such and such passages

gray whiteness of fog against top of shadowed ridge

line of ten pelicans gliding above mouth of channel

8.29

light coming into clouds above still shadowed ridge

circular orange flower below sandstone-colored wall

object of others left to others but part of another

connections between them based on two kinds of same

possibilities of multiple self and its voices sites

and settings of words in some undisclosed locations

gray whiteness of clouds by black shoulder of ridge

pelican gliding to the left toward mouth of channel

8.30

blue pink yellows of sky above still shadowed ridge

motionless black pine branches across redwood fence

first opposed how something is at the same time not

shadows somewhere on the face of the building below

woman recalling being born 4 minutes after midnight

mother saying person who recorded the time was slow

edge of fog moving in above black shoulder of ridge

pelican gliding to the left across mouth of channel

8.31

fog moving to the left against still shadowed ridge

sound of bird chirping on branch in left foreground

this would be physically similar to one another and

width from 0 to one of the surfaces said to be that

woman recalling moving enormous Cecile Brunner rose

before bulldozers still blooms now at 100 years old

edge of sun rising into fog against invisible ridge

white line of wave breaking on sand next to channel

9.1

light gray whiteness of fog against invisible ridge

motionless green bamboo leaves across redwood fence

attention to flow of ideas in that paper circulated

shape of table as much as lines perspective reverse

shape on page sound in air whose meanings intersect

in the time it takes for words to be read and heard

gray whiteness of fog still against invisible ridge

white line of wave breaking on sand next to channel

9.2

blue pink yellow of sky beside still shadowed ridge

motionless green of leaves on branches beside fence

first before completing painting simplified concern

sound which has shattered itself even sounding here

any one possible sounding of sequence cicada cicada

cicada cicada produces an amphibrach hexameter line

cloudless blue white sky above black plane of ridge

line of pelicans gliding to the left toward channel

9.3

first light coming into fog against invisible ridge

motionless black branches above fence in foreground

still makes the small number of forms it might take

both to think and draw at same time eye sharp focus

many hours of looking and working a moment elements

come together action throwing objects up in the air

gray blackness of fog against still invisible ridge

line of white lights on horizon across from channel

9.4

light gray whiteness of fog against invisible ridge

sound of birds chirping in field in left foreground

position close to eliminate brings it into presence

location too what matters picture itself a question

one hopes for a mourning dove on the apex of a roof

being when thinking of Autumn this place also whole

gray whiteness of fog against still invisible ridge

white line of wave breaking on sand next to channel

9.5

clouds moving to the right above blackness of ridge

motion of shadowed green bamboo leaves across fence

clock could be at rest relative to motion of system

other condition normal to different unit of measure

picture moving left to right across fog above ridge

little luminous strips of light beside fog on water

lighter lower edge of cloud above shoulder of ridge

sunlit white terns circling toward mouth of channel

9.6

light in window opposite unmade yellow and blue bed

motionless green bamboo leaves across redwood fence

conversations of group continued for full six years

grid had managed to converge to the vanishing point

heard it against a sometimes wall of sound by often

several voices going simultaneously one was hearing

gray whiteness of fog against still invisible ridge

line of pelicans gliding to the left toward channel

9.7

dream in unmade yellow and blue bed opposite window

mother younger stepped out of shower naked shoulder

concern with contrast of color after making drawing

there which was itself saying more than all that is

appearing here as a yellow smiling face in the moon

without which whatever was said was somehow looking

gray whiteness of clouds against top of black ridge

pelicans gliding to the left above mouth of channel

9.8

cloudless blue white sky above black plane of ridge

motion of shadowed green bamboo leaves across fence

more even if left to choice would still be speaking

feel in the 4th term form element basis of painting

sister brings home a mourning dove having been shot

stands on perch for years talking to self in mirror

pale blue whiteness of sky beside shoulder of ridge

white line of wave breaking across mouth of channel

9.9

dream in unmade yellow and blue bed opposite window

man holding onto a ledge below top of vertical wall

opposed to which as look there first emerges moment

present self as "level" speaks sense of the horizon

recalls being given too much morphine after surgery

wakes up saying good Lord put me on holding pattern

cloudless blue white sky by black shoulder of ridge

shadowed swell lines moving toward mouth of channel

9.10

cloudless blue pink yellow of sky above black ridge

sound of jet passing over pine branch in foreground

could be system at rest relative to state of motion

direction fixed in space from ways we imagine point

days filled with clouds blue patch of sky starlings

whistling from a tree a small plane passes overhead

cloudless blue white sky by black shoulder of ridge

white line of wave breaking across mouth of channel

9.11

fog moving to the left in pale blue sky above ridge

sparrow hopping across bricks next to redwood fence

when he was twenty-three in less surrounding ground

to look back at objects looking back at camera seen

minimal application of form and color topographical

view of remembered things seen rather than imagined

gray whiteness of fog against top of shadowed ridge

swell line moving toward windblown mouth of channel

9.12

light coming into sky above shadowed plane of ridge

motionless green bamboo leaves beside redwood fence

August was done "more or less" between each present

these one more breath from which we have quoted end

question of being now become this is how it happens

itself between the sense of no longer comes to pass

pink red orange sky next to black shoulder of ridge

white lines of waves breaking into mouth of channel

9.13

pink lines of clouds in bright blue sky above ridge

shadowed green leaves on branch above redwood fence

see myself as others see me one after another seems

other past and present elements a form of structure

something about front view in sculpture the unknown

always behind us fog a picture turns it upside down

line of jet trail slanting across shoulder of ridge

white line of wave breaking on sand next to channel

9.14

light coming into blue whiteness of sky above ridge

sound of unseen towhee chirping in right foreground

to bring into concealed names the removal of a word

ordinary man's forearm in trying to sound the alarm

woman on left carrying boy out of classroom yelling

legs kicking teacher standing there holding a snake

blinding whiteness of sun next to shoulder of ridge

shadowed swell lines moving toward mouth of channel

9.15

light coming into fog against still invisible ridge

white circle of moon beside shadowed black branches

time of an event given relative to length in motion

line running through point responding to line there

long line reaching clear across the horizontal page

temporal fact of shifts from one moment to the next

pink cloud in pale blue sky above fog against ridge

shadowed white line of wave breaking across channel

9.16

gray whiteness of clouds above shadowed green ridge

circular pink roses next to corner of redwood fence

dating back to traditional use of color and systems

impression of structure in space evidence of things

darkness in which things gather in their uniqueness

as light-ray of thinking radiates untraversed space

shadowed light gray cloud against shoulder of ridge

diagonal white line of wave breaking across channel

9.17

light in window opposite unmade yellow and blue bed

motion of shadowed green leaves above redwood fence

describe drawing as the position of certain figures

another breath a mouth become thought of moving air

color also "correct" system according to procedures

still seen in series begins resting in a small room

whiteness of jet trail in pale blue sky above ridge

white line of wave breaking across mouth of channel

9.18

light gray rain cloud against still invisible ridge

sparrows standing on edge of shadowed redwood fence

sense which follows and brings to light the absence

tension belonging to accident consideration of same

house built on the water granite cliffs not eroding

now that he has gone she doesn't want to live there

gray rain cloud against top of still shadowed ridge

line of pelicans gliding to the left toward channel

9.19

light in cloudless blue sky above still black ridge

waning white moon beside rose branch across from it

concealed "closure" ambiguous on the one hand first

person in water sea level of everything at the edge

throwing a basket of flowers over railing into blue

blue sea ship sailing enroute Yokohama to Hong Kong

pale orange of sky above shadowed shoulder of ridge

pelican gliding to the left toward mouth of channel

9.20

light coming into blue blackness of sky above ridge

waning white moon next to rose branch in foreground

interval parallel to other based on two assumptions

this amount taken from any fixed start to end point

as poised balanced on the point between one present

thought surrounded by one penumbral feeling another

blinding whiteness of sun next to still black ridge

line of pelicans flapping to the right toward point

9.21

dream in unmade yellow and blue bed opposite window

walking across chaos of rocks where sand used to be

color also "correct" system according to procedures

still seen in series begins resting in a small room

feeling one has when a person comes in walks around

the far side of the room between you and its window

bright circle of sun rising above shoulder of ridge

shadowed white wave breaking on sand beside channel

9.22

gray whiteness of fog against still invisible ridge

sound of birds chirping from branches in foreground

done on the spot did not return the site of details

everything ever thought would still be first of all

man recalling a gout attack on Molokai doctor gives

Oxycodone makes everything just a little bit better

gray whiteness of fog still against invisible ridge

edge of white wave breaking on sand next to channel

9.23

light coming into fog against still invisible ridge

faint white curve of moon through fog beside branch

thought in part to open time set back to the moment

work basic subject matter examines form and content

strangely resonant since it all takes place present

always disappearing becomes past soon as it happens

gray whiteness of fog still against invisible ridge

white line of wave breaking on sand next to channel

9.24

first light coming into sky above still black ridge

upturned curve of thin white moon above pine branch

then also place on the other hand concealed absence

calm about how from level to level various surfaces

pieces of glass embedded in man's left index finger

the body laid out on the table having been violated

pale red orange sky next to black shoulder of ridge

shadowed white line of wave breaking across channel

9.25

horizontal red orange cloud above still black ridge

curve of waning white moon across from black branch

different twice by the time it follows simultaneous

point on line as function of time note first second

words going forth toward revelation itself as it is

shapes can be written at same time as what they say

sunlit pink red cloud above black shoulder of ridge

line of pelicans gliding to the left toward channel

9.26

light coming into fog against still invisible ridge

streaked sparrow walking across bricks beside fence

when young did not attempt later contrast to itself

one week goes by shows room which contains a window

woman recalling walking each day to school bus stop

followed by two goats called Mr. Johnson and Easter

gray whiteness of fog still against invisible ridge

line of pelicans gliding to the left toward channel

9.27

light coming into cloud in front of invisible ridge

motionless black pine branches across redwood fence

could instead be the fact which had served as model

noticeable measure of difference nature of language

example for one thing how last two lines transcribe

something seen when out there in water at eye level

gray rain cloud against invisible shoulder of ridge

diagonal white line of wave breaking across channel

9.28

blue pink yellow of sky beside black plane of ridge

sparrows standing on edge of shadowed redwood fence

preceding the making even while suspend time's flow

these determined by external present form and color

recalling paintings by Rousseau Vincent and Cézanne

followed by Rothko Still Kelly Matisse and Mondrian

blinding white edge of sun beside shoulder of ridge

line of 5 pelicans flapping toward mouth of channel

9.29

first light coming into sky above still black ridge

wind moving through bamboo leaves across from fence

looking which points out falling away from position

surface shades to the left sometimes a line of blue

listener hearing voice reading turns around someone

standing there eyes closed picture going into ocean

pale red orange sky next to black shoulder of ridge

shadowed white line of wave breaking across channel

9.30

vertical gray cloud moving to the right above ridge

song sparrow calling from pine branch in foreground

event of distance between two points follows motion

different with respect to names appropriate calling

moon sits here in empty sky beside star glows there

behind from what appears to be swiftly moving water

gray plane of cloud next to black shoulder of ridge

diagonal white line of wave breaking across channel

10.1

light coming into blue blackness of sky above ridge

sound of bird chirping on branch in left foreground

pieces which surround him painting drawn from those

ceiling made by central light margin in perspective

one thing after another coming up wanting paintings

done at once blond girl in red convertible laughing

cloudless red orange of sky above shoulder of ridge

shadowed white line of wave breaking across channel

10.2

light coming into cloudless blue of sky above ridge

motionless black branches above fence in foreground

some still complete before many differences in view

some who were more say for this one breath by which

words going forth toward revelation itself as it is

shapes can be written at same time as what they say

blue pink yellows of sky by black shoulder of ridge

white line of wave breaking across mouth of channel

10.3

first light coming into sky above still black ridge

motionless bamboo leaves above fence across from it

moment of a situation closed which is already there

construct sources of painting purpose and structure

renewal of activities every morning resolutely this

following that and these each day looking listening

reddish orange of sky above black shoulder of ridge

shadowed swell lines moving toward mouth of channel

10.4

light coming into blue blackness of sky above ridge

wind moving through shadowed bamboo leaves by fence

absence here beside concealed would be another name

sometime the level of the far side of less and less

each day events interwoven nothing more than itself

insisting on hanging around beyond an ordinary life

pale red orange sky next to black shoulder of ridge

line of pelicans gliding to the left toward channel

10.5

faint whiteness of stars above black plane of ridge

motionless black bamboo leaves beside redwood fence

follow in two scales made when applied to formation

calling in the direction of line therefore in space

"apple" isn't another apple over there somewhere in

real space but has its own reality here on the page

light coming into sky above black shoulder of ridge

orange line of light on horizon across from channel

10.6

bright whiteness of star in predawn sky above ridge

sound of water falling on rocks in right foreground

piece at every turn in contrast to beginning change

sets out in the margin toward narrowed part of room

man in blue shirt perhaps enough to materialize him

what lingers awhile delays it persist in hanging on

sunlit red orange corner of triangular granite peak

shadowed green branches of trees on ridge beside it

10.7

pink white edge of cloud above still shadowed ridge

sounds of sparrows calling from field in foreground

time of day and other shadows figures to be thought

more not just saying rather this one breath another

comes about on any page in the original translation

seems to be happening in reading what is being said

blinding white circle of sun in cloud next to ridge

shadowed swell lines moving toward mouth of channel

10.8

gray whiteness of fog against still invisible ridge

motionless green bamboo leaves beside redwood fence

why it so often happens that after giving up a plan

extract from letter following an apparent beginning

imprint of living hand moving pen across page makes

letters real as the physical things they talk about

gray whiteness of fog still against invisible ridge

white line of wave breaking on sand next to channel

10.9

first light coming into sky above still black ridge

sparrows pecking up seeds from bricks in foreground

reflection in far-reaching sight reveals it against

one thinks about it looking down on it how far back

blue-eyed window moves toward something all at once

expanding the moment inside out into somewhere else

red orange sky beside still black shoulder of ridge

shadowed swell lines moving toward mouth of channel

10.10

light pink edge of cloudless blue sky next to ridge

wind moving through bamboo leaves across from fence

part of light which referred to different direction

there as is now seen has points in common with line

woman across table talking about moving toward edge

clear to horizon light pink flower on a blue ground

cloudless pink yellow sky next to shoulder of ridge

shadowed swell lines moving across mouth of channel

10.11

first light coming into sky above still black ridge

motionless black pine branch by fence in foreground

all his work begins with a landscape painted others

where perpendicular run down far corner to end wall

mixed up Robinson Crusoe narrative of a shipwrecked

sailor who lived for years on small tropical island

orange circle of sun rising above shoulder of ridge

line of four pelicans gliding across toward channel

10.12

light in window opposite unmade yellow and blue bed

sound of crow calling on branch in right foreground

early letter sketch of sand on paper image just now

breath saying other than the rest of saying nothing

sounds in themselves without relation to each other

one's being at home in words through world as sound

blinding white edge of sun beside shoulder of ridge

cormorants flapping to the right toward the horizon

10.13

moonlit blackness of sky above black plane of ridge

white circle of moon next to branches in foreground

feeling of after all that matter of form from start

no longer possible to locate a copy of the original

man writing VT green NOV black EMBER red WOODS blue

not pathetic but pastoral fallacy pretty well drawn

gray blackness of sky above black shoulder of ridge

white circle of moon above clouds across from point

10.14

gray whiteness of clouds above black plane of ridge

motion of shadowed green bamboo leaves across fence

itself for and against through which it falls apart

physical spaces there relative to optical phenomena

can almost see white feel cold right outside window

warm here in the house what with fire still glowing

sunlit white edge of clouds above shoulder of ridge

diagonal white line of wave breaking across channel

10.15

light gray whiteness of fog against invisible ridge

sparrows pecking up seeds from bricks next to fence

green grass seen above looking more and more things

whose "front" and "back" is called the direction of

one thing followed by another occupied with what is

going on days shorter moving toward end of the year

gray whiteness of fog against still invisible ridge

line of pelicans gliding to the left toward channel

10.16

light in window opposite unmade yellow and blue bed

white circle of moon by clouds across from branches

begins about between when he left instead immediate

where ground verticals turn whole ceiling into room

man on blue board dropping into wave hits head sand

comes up electric pain neck back shoulders fracture

red orange yellow of clouds above shoulder of ridge

wingspan of bird flapping to the right toward point

10.17

dream in unmade yellow and blue bed opposite window

man tucking under breaking ledge of blue green wave

letter seen from above pink tinge with violet water

saying says the sound of word which invisibly space

diagonal red orange shaft of sunlight against ridge

sound of wave in still motionless channel breathing

shadowed line of cloud in pale blue sky above ridge

wingspan of bird flapping to the right toward point

10.18

pink edge of light in cloud above still black ridge

waning white moon beside rose branch across from it

see will act the part in a way that comes to be one

one become among other things black and white color

sun above the mountain red and green and blue looks

out the kitchen window here cold wind blowing there

pink redness of cloud above black shoulder of ridge

shadowed white line of wave breaking across channel

10.19

pink red orange of cloud above black plane of ridge

sound of red-shouldered hawk calling across from it

here through which it falls and out of which begins

level of wall even in the distant thinking about it

line ending in that these simple geometrical shapes

space on page registers world of perception thought

pale orange plane of clouds above shoulder of ridge

shadowed swell lines moving toward mouth of channel

10.20

cloudless blue red orange yellow of sky above ridge

two crows flapping to the right over black branches

relative to earth as body influenced by velocity of

points in common with straight line vision of whole

view of point part thinking it first in speaking of

view of name moves in the sphere of what is evident

blue white pale orange sky beside shoulder of ridge

shadowed white line of wave breaking across channel

10.21

light coming into blue whiteness of sky above ridge

shadowed towhee standing on corner of redwood fence

all who saw painting as much as he could first hand

four drawings following temporarily stilled content

ridge being there in these same words every morning

now see in mind's eye as photo of paintings in show

yellow orange edge of sky next to shoulder of ridge

shadowed swell lines moving toward mouth of channel

10.22

white line of cloud in blue black sky next to ridge

motion of shadowed green bamboo leaves beside fence

bright green sky color unloading drawing it as well

inner space the ear first follow what is to be said

pen in hand forms letters the alphabet of the world

follows eye and ear sensing what one sees and hears

red yellow orange of sky above black plane of ridge

shadowed line of swell approaching mouth of channel

10.23

light in cloudless blue black sky above black ridge

upturned curve of waning moon to the left of branch

act which is in something in order to go against it

these colors in consequence of following reflection

disparate cloud colors opening into expanded moment

converging in field of light at the edge of the sun

blue pink red yellow orange edge of sky above ridge

shadowed swell lines moving toward mouth of channel

10.24

first light in cloudless blue black sky above ridge

white curve of moon above motion of shadowed bamboo

think and speak less about this more than beginning

construct some kind of point sometimes out of joint

something can appear in the reaching out of subject

kind of one which here ground out of which anything

blue pink red yellow of sky above shoulder of ridge

swell line moving across windblown mouth of channel

10.25

light in window opposite unmade yellow and blue bed

upturned curve of waning moon next to pine branches

those known can hardly be doubled on the other hand

vision already carried last branch parallel to axes

matter itself in the same way as absence everywhere

shows the physical occurrences with respect to view

red orange line of cloud by black shoulder of ridge

shadowed swell lines moving toward mouth of channel

10.26

lower edge of blue white sky next to shadowed ridge

shadowed bird slanting toward green glass back door

mentioned together with divisions forms of painting

man standing before rectangular doors windows frame

something can appear in the reaching out of subject

kind of one which here ground out of which anything

yellow red orange of sky by black shoulder of ridge

shadowed line of swell approaching mouth of channel

10.27

cloudless blue white sky above black plane of ridge

wind moving into shadowed bamboo leaves above fence

letter put this drawing of a picture unloading sand

song belonging to whole drawn draft of wind unheard

rhythm of ongoing writing it down every day so that

attention to which something might actually be seen

yellow red orange sky above black shoulder of ridge

shadowed swell line moving across windblown channel

10.28

pale reddish line of clouds above still black ridge

motionless black bamboo leaves beside redwood fence

forward something called by it vertical or slanting

volume translated by letter to elements of painting

connect to shape and color on two-dimensional plane

maybe those clouds will turn red once sun goes down

blue red yellow edge of sky above shoulder of ridge

diagonal swell lines moving toward mouth of channel

10.29

white edge of pale blue sky above still black ridge

motionless black bamboo leaves beside redwood fence

that therefore in thinking back into or beyond this

sometimes commentary on one thing in a sense moment

on the other hand unrecognized occurrence of ground

thinking "of" being here hidden in pressing present

blue pink yellow orange sky above shoulder of ridge

diagonal swell lines moving toward mouth of channel

10.30

first light in cloudless blue black sky above ridge

motion of wind in black bamboo leaves next to fence

optical problems moving bodies in light of observed

space acts at a point where velocity may be changed

first reading about moire patterns later seeing one

wind-driven lines of wave approach mouth of channel

blue yellow pink red edge of sky beside black ridge

swell line moving across windblown mouth of channel

10.31

first light coming into sky above still black ridge

motionless black pine branches beside redwood fence

early as a point of seeing drawn close to immediate

rectangular focus simultaneous question of the room

look at red flower against the green grown in a pot

outside apartment in Mexico continue a conversation

smoke red orange sky beside black shoulder of ridge

shadowed line of swell approaching mouth of channel

11.1

light in window opposite unmade yellow and blue bed

faint white stars in blackness of sky next to ridge

see drawing close to a figure place in another hand

said of wind breath followed by what is kept silent

action of ongoing writing it down every day so that

attention to which something might actually be seen

reddish orange edge of sky beside shoulder of ridge

shadowed swell lines moving toward windless channel

11.2

blue pink yellow of sky beside still shadowed ridge

motion of green bamboo leaves next to redwood fence

obstacles to rock face things which for one subject

statement in color translated by subject to letters

arbitrariness by which letters may break into words

phenomena of world unfolded in time as one notes it

blinding white edge of sun beside shoulder of ridge

white line of wave breaking on sand next to channel

11.3

first light in cloudless blue black sky above ridge

sound of owl hooing from branch in right foreground

beginning here of what is saying thought setting up

sense another says painting to keep things changing

sometimes miraculous detonations of thought repeats

shape on page frames things happening early morning

blue pink yellow of sky beside still shadowed ridge

shadowed swell line in otherwise motionless channel

11.4

dream in unmade yellow and blue bed opposite window

Edwin Dobb walks back in as if nothing had happened

phenomena in double sequence of light with velocity

statement in cases when system of reference changed

if you just disappear and no one talks about it how

do you explain what you did in the physical present

gray whiteness of fog against still invisible ridge

white line of wave breaking on sand next to channel

11.5

light coming into fog against still invisible ridge

sound of bird calling on branch in right foreground

closest to most recent called as it was taking form

mirror seen within which seeing takes place outside

angle of house or bird calling colors equal to view

person seen from behind when the viewer isn't there

gray whiteness of fog still against invisible ridge

white line of wave breaking on sand next to channel

11.6

gray whiteness of fog against still invisible ridge

sound of crow calling on branch in right foreground

reed pen and graphite on paper inscribed to his son

the more some turn to the open call its whole sound

someone looking back recalls what happened that day

moment of being there is witness to things now gone

gray white fog against still invisible top of ridge

swell line approaching otherwise motionless channel

11.7

light coming into fog against still invisible ridge

house sparrows perched on fence in right foreground

one who projects such forms from the mass of things

direction of line and letter in revised translation

perhaps no more than an extended desire to document

bird standing on redwood fence before it disappears

light gray whiteness of fog against invisible ridge

white line of wave breaking across mouth of channel

11.8

light coming into fog against still invisible ridge

sound of bird chirping on branch in left foreground

saying to get this beginning of the story to follow

lamps going on once logic of light in the left hand

listener who can't make out what the words are will

still hear their essential tone pause pitch silence

gray whiteness of fog still against invisible ridge

shadowed line of swell approaching mouth of channel

11.9

light gray whiteness of fog against invisible ridge

song sparrows lined up on fence in right foreground

explained therefore according to every other system

field where force transforms space in such way that

environment appears to be encoded with significance

hummingbird approaching flower across from listener

gray whiteness of fog against still invisible ridge

white edge of wave breaking on sand next to channel

11.10

light in window opposite unmade yellow and blue bed

first bird chirping from branch in right foreground

paint emphasized by light and dark broad flat color

active for example structure held in place by force

one attending to what's on one level familiar world

shifting light observed meaning logic of difference

gray whiteness of fog against top of shadowed ridge

diagonal white line of wave breaking across channel

11.11

cloudless blue pink white edge of sky next to ridge

two sparrows landing on feeder beside redwood fence

only until part placed between attention to letters

these recall the part against objective inner space

transcription of these things actions events taking

place in world out there word as enactment of world

fog moving across still invisible shoulder of ridge

shadowed line of swell approaching mouth of channel

11.12

first light coming into fog against invisible ridge

white-crowned sparrow landing on feeder below fence

then nothing except those it set in form of subject

references contained in given note follows document

each thing is first of all itself in order to exist

likewise these words the manifestation of something

light coming into fog against still invisible ridge

white edge of wave breaking on sand next to channel

11.13

light blue whiteness of fog against invisible ridge

motionless black pine branch next to shadowed fence

word following third direct thinking position limit

tree visible even when the picture is more and more

think about horizon line taking photo look at ridge

pine tree in right corner shifted so it isn't there

light gray whiteness of fog against invisible ridge

white line of wave breaking across mouth of channel

11.14

light coming into clouds above shadowed green ridge

two sparrows landing on feeder beside redwood fence

consequence of physical time it follows from before

where point divided remains unchanged called moment

relation between visual actions and events in place

horizontal timeline passing by in these three shots

gray whiteness of clouds above still shadowed ridge

diagonal white line of wave breaking across channel

11.15

gray blue whiteness of sky beside still black ridge

blue jay standing on edge of shadowed redwood fence

area called present painting view a tree-lined road

last drawing furthest thought about vision of field

see what one sees out the window driving down there

overlook series of three pictures one looking south

blinding whiteness of sun next to cloud above ridge

shadowed line of swell approaching mouth of channel

11.16

dream in unmade yellow and blue bed opposite window

mattresses on ground floor of building fire burning

often featured as record differences in such detail

hear recalling the hand who says more of the object

if out of nothing something allows such possibility

word being able to say what presents itself to show

gray whiteness of fog against still invisible ridge

white edge of wave breaking on sand next to channel

11.17

white lines of clouds in pale blue sky beside ridge

motionless green bamboo leaves above shadowed fence

external world coming to light in things and action

notes appearance thought to be located with subject

something about places location coming out of place

also turns out to be sense of duration time passing

blinding whiteness of sun next to shoulder of ridge

shadowed swell lines moving toward mouth of channel

11.18

cloudless blue white sky above still shadowed ridge

almost half moon next to rose branch across from it

position related to likewise focusing on glimpse of

yellow as if it will never let go aspect of picture

writing down something seen from water at eye level

pelicans flapping out of fog toward tip of sandspit

yellow orange circle of sun above shoulder of ridge

waning edge of moon next to NO PARKING ANYTIME sign

11.19

dream in unmade yellow and blue bed opposite window

something about remembering going surfing every day

coordinates with respect to measure of rigid bodies

mass passing through motion of point look of moment

physical position which remains absent occurs since

beginning of story announcing itself against an end

edge of reddish gray cloud beside shoulder of ridge

shadowed line of swell approaching mouth of channel

11.20

curve of gray cloud in blue white sky next to ridge

whiteness of moon by leaves on branches above fence

resembles painting trees made of shapes contrasting

depth of apparent intervals place of vanishing line

girl in yellow dress whose left hand reaches branch

other hand holds up ballet slipper with hole in toe

yellow red orange edge of sky beside shadowed ridge

shadowed line of swell approaching mouth of channel

11.21

light coming into cloudless blue white sky by ridge

whiteness of waning moon next to leaves on branches

missing stars and branch much earlier than painting

called one in a different way remains in this sense

woman in green sweater standing by green front door

her sister having just seen eagle landing on branch

blinding yellow edge of sun above shoulder of ridge

shadowed swell lines moving toward mouth of channel

11.22

gray plane of cloud in blue white sky next to ridge

motion of shadowed green bamboo leaves beside fence

things in the active sense would seem between which

references appear to rest on see for example answer

yellow orange of sun reflected in nearly motionless

channel suggests the position of invisible observer

blinding white sun comes up above shoulder of ridge

white curve of moon next to NO PARKING ANYTIME sign

11.23

cloudless blue white sky above still shadowed ridge

waning white moon next to leaves on bamboo branches

what it has concealed might be such that it becomes

try to forget or see if in the coming weeks certain

every day moves into the flow of continuous present

moment an occurrence of what happens to be that day

blinding white edge of sun beside shoulder of ridge

shadowed line of swell approaching mouth of channel

11.24

cloudless blue white sky above black plane of ridge

faint white curve of moon across from bamboo branch

measurements present somewhere event whose distance

consequence of the other above therefore depends on

someone inside room remembers things to fix eyes on

sometimes one's mind choked with material disbelief

orange edge of sun comes up above shoulder of ridge

shadowed white line of wave breaking across channel

11.25

diagonal line of cloud in pale blue sky above ridge

motion of bamboo leaves in wind above redwood fence

resembled modulated tones of the road seen up close

leaving the room traversed by network of deep space

rhythm of ongoing writing it down every day so that

attention to which something might actually be seen

first yellow edge of sun above still shadowed ridge

swell line moving toward windblown mouth of channel

11.26

light pink red cloud in pale blue sky next to ridge

silhouette of sparrow landing on edge redwood fence

probably September from which it differs in details

answer sooner which draws to itself the whole draft

one thing followed by another occupied with what is

going on days shorter moving toward end of the year

sun rising into yellow red orange sky next to ridge

shadowed swell lines moving toward mouth of channel

11.27

gray rain cloud above still shadowed plane of ridge

house sparrow landing on feeder in right foreground

outside possible beyond which point things would be

see translation to locate the original of statement

therefore given present things visible when and how

one remains at the same time has relation to ground

shaft of light slanting down from cloud above ridge

white line of wave breaking across mouth of channel

11.28

gray plane of clouds in pale blue sky against ridge

crow flapping from the left above black pine branch

follow the word "concealed" brings to our attention

gray and brown tones seem to recede into the ground

picture postcard sugar cane plantations clouds come

bring rain to island green blue water strange names

white edge of sun rising above clouds against ridge

shadowed line of swell approaching mouth of channel

11.29

gray shape of cloud in blue white sky next to ridge

white-crowned sparrow landing on bricks below fence

from there to compare time the event with the clock

removal of expression comes out clearly in this way

sunlit yellow redness of apples on branches of tree

how hard it is here to imagine them not being there

yellow white edges of cloud above shoulder of ridge

shadowed white line of wave breaking across channel

11.30

light gray whiteness of clouds above shadowed ridge

sparrows pecking up seeds from bricks next to fence

trees as bright light verticals form pattern across

perspective pulls it forward line both near and far

long shadowed lines beginning to fall across sunlit

grasses in field white cloud in pale blue white sky

light gray rain cloud above black shoulder of ridge

shadowed white wave breaking into windblown channel

12.1

gray rain cloud moving across top of shadowed ridge

motion of windblown green bamboo leaves above fence

described simply as sketch rather than afterthought

some of those who say more closed off visible space

this tree those clouds that long grassy slope keeps

coming back in another glance at next day's weather

gray rain cloud against invisible shoulder of ridge

whiteness of waves breaking across mouth of channel

12.2

light gray rain cloud against still invisible ridge

two sparrows landing on feeder beside redwood fence

reflect the same action if not measured in terms of

references not appear to have been included however

letter to brother Harper Oregon three hours writing

every morning rest of day filled with making garden

gray of rain clouds moving across shoulder of ridge

windblown whiteness of wave breaking across channel

12.3

light coming into clouds above black plane of ridge

planet below shadowed black pine branch above fence

area where original colors green strokes dark brown

experience even less explicitly thought of as found

diagonal pale orange lines of light slanting across

sun rising above shoulder of ridge forward thinking

gray plane of clouds in pale blue sky next to ridge

shadowed swell line moving across windblown channel

12.4

first gray light in rain cloud against top of ridge

motion of windblown green of shadowed bamboo leaves

time of light in place at point of rest relative to

direction for system of reference on the other hand

pain in one's left hand after father's hand surgery

letting sister go back to Australia speaking of now

light gray rain cloud against top of shadowed ridge

white lines of waves breaking into mouth of channel

12.5

pink red edge of cloud in pale blue sky above ridge

3 sparrows standing on feeder next to redwood fence

areas in manner of another view glance at landscape

loops a finger about the line space vanishing point

crawl space under kitchen gets down to about a foot

excavation just to get to the damaged areas exposed

pale pink red edge of cloud above shoulder of ridge

wingspan of vulture flapping by branch toward point

12.6

light coming into clouds above black plane of ridge

shapes of black bamboo leaves on branch above fence

such a view of making interest in the subject color

who appears becomes visible orbit some who are more

profile of dog in tuxedo on porch shiplapped siding

white paint shadow of panes in window you don't see

yellow red orange of cloud beside shoulder of ridge

wingspan of vulture gliding above windblown channel

12.7

light gray rain cloud moving across invisible ridge

sparrow landing on redwood fence across from feeder

beyond which things would appear not to be possible

white cloud dark wood letter otherwise unless noted

A black BAT green A red BAT blue buzzed by two bats

making it feel like it's happening here on the page

light gray rain cloud against still invisible ridge

windblown gulls gliding to the right toward horizon

12.8

sunlit white clouds in blue white sky next to ridge

sparrows lined up on edge of shadowed redwood fence

previous features let us see what we can see appear

in the middle ranges woman with basket on far shore

something over and over again as object and subject

between which to someone who appeared to be turning

white circle of sun coming up in clouds above ridge

shadowed swell lines moving toward mouth of channel

12.9

first light in sky above still black plane of ridge

blue jay standing on edge of shadowed redwood fence

following light sent out from instant when distance

system of motion structure in such a way that place

first comes one who has turned such objects present

places itself where said forgetting the consequence

red orange line of cloud by black shoulder of ridge

shadowed swell lines moving toward mouth of channel

12.10

dream in unmade yellow and blue bed opposite window

how about to ski down steep white slope phone rings

hills and a house enough to resemble tonal contrast

simultaneous space projected as visual toward sight

wants to shape the outline of what needs to be done

keeps on doing whatever it is in the world one does

red orange of clouds beside black shoulder of ridge

shadowed swell lines moving across windless channel

12.11

gray white rain cloud against still invisible ridge

sparrow standing on shadowed bamboo branch by fence

light in letters during time given in separate view

experience the way song traces the sound calling it

man in blue shirt walking down from balcony reading

wanting letters and words to be entirely themselves

gray rain cloud against invisible shoulder of ridge

line of pelicans gliding to the left toward channel

12.12

first light coming into fog against invisible ridge

silhouette of bird landing on edge of redwood fence

here makes its appearance in order to stand against

letters given to look situation beginning to change

each sentence balanced on the comma's central point

ridge in relation to sky motion of cloud against it

gray whiteness of fog against still invisible ridge

white edge of wave breaking on sand next to channel

12.13

first light coming into fog against invisible ridge

motionless black pine branches across redwood fence

first in doing is now more than ever something does

again putting these things to say about time of day

squirreled away under a lamp on the couch in living

room wanting to give an account of what one's doing

gray whiteness of fog against still invisible ridge

white line of wave breaking across mouth of channel

12.14

diagonal line of cloud in pale blue sky above ridge

waning white circle of moon above shadowed branches

following light the time of events which take place

different becomes in this which does not contradict

addition expanded into the present would be changed

subject still more physical which happens to forget

red orange of clouds beside black shoulder of ridge

shadowed line of swell approaching mouth of channel

12.15

cloudless blue white sky above black plane of ridge

white circle of moon by tip of shadowed rose branch

landscapes more than in later years period remained

space the ways home again the occupied room resumed

looks at four year old girl swimming pool in Mexico

shadowed green parrot perched on an upturned branch

orange edge of sun rising next to shoulder of ridge

lines of birds flapping to the right toward horizon

12.16

horizontal lines of clouds beside still black ridge

waning white circle of moon by tip of rose branches

details the opposition to day and night see concept

draws some trace of the track in sound that is said

two views of almost half moon above shadowed leaves

after noting scale substitutes for depth perception

yellow red orange sky above black shoulder of ridge

parallel swell lines moving toward mouth of channel

12.17

gray white of sky beside still black plane of ridge

sparrows standing on edge of shadowed redwood fence

ground which is almost entirely absent in this case

see in part between reader and position of thinking

person remembering street in Ismir gun aimed at her

back someone placing bomb behind tire of Ford truck

red orange edges of cloud next to shoulder of ridge

shadowed line of swell approaching mouth of channel

12.18

dream in unmade yellow and blue bed opposite window

something about man in uniform rain falling on roof

measure horizon of facts what is said here about it

think to get into focus see version turning between

moon at last coming out behind clouds so huge there

here too goes down behind trees now not quite round

gray rain cloud moving across top of shadowed ridge

white wave breaking into windblown mouth of channel

12.19

light coming into clouds above black plane of ridge

motion of bamboo leaves in wind above redwood fence

velocity of event in time relates to system at rest

maybe in a manner exemplified by indicating effects

form whose numbers measure present remaining absent

action in present brings about appearances possible

shaft of light slanting down from cloud above ridge

diagonal white line of wave breaking across channel

12.20

light coming into blue blackness of sky above ridge

waning white curve of moon beside shadowed branches

view of landscapes familiar with numerous paintings

in some ways interior even more than absorbed space

black curve of branches in landscape moves backward

picture a plane of color and light shadow in motion

pinkish red of clouds above black shoulder of ridge

white curve of moon next to NO PARKING ANYTIME sign

12.21

gray whiteness of clouds above green plane of ridge

song sparrow landing on feeder beside redwood fence

scene conceived in reed pen character letter sketch

arrive at the song that sings beginning point where

Ella Fitzgerald's singing contends with a ceaseless

back and forth pounding of one's upstairs neighbors

pink redness of cloud above black shoulder of ridge

whiteness of wave breaking across windblown channel

12.22

light gray rain cloud against still invisible ridge

rufous-sided towhee on bricks next to redwood fence

everywhere but equal in the name of idea has become

following this given present factual description of

black curve of branches in landscape moves backward

picture a plane of color and light shadow in motion

gray rain cloud against invisible shoulder of ridge

gulls gliding to the right across windblown channel

12.23

horizontal line of cloud above still shadowed ridge

white curve of moon in bamboo branches beside fence

what if on the contrary horizon let beginning be it

between the calm of dissonance resolved by means of

horizon line in a fogbank so you can't quite see it

imagine the rocks in Utah being washed into the sea

cloudless blue sky above cloud by shoulder of ridge

shadowed swell lines moving toward mouth of channel

12.24

white lines of clouds in blue white sky above ridge

sparrows pecking up seeds from feeder next to fence

definition which made the time not follow from this

point in a kind of motion according to line of such

when you're living in the present moment things are

noticing everything sort of just there is happening

pale yellow orange of sky next to shoulder of ridge

shadowed line of swell approaching mouth of channel

12.25

light coming into clouds above still shadowed ridge

sparrows pecking up seeds from feeder next to fence

having seen the above-mentioned possible antecedent

continuing show the position without having to move

windblown cypress tree on upturned curve of horizon

moving closer to viewer whose position doesn't move

pink red of clouds in sky next to shoulder of ridge

shadowed swell lines moving toward mouth of channel

12.26

cloudless blue white sky above still shadowed ridge

wind moving bamboo leaves on branches next to fence

graphite details such as wood on the floor resolved

saying the kind of answers to the time of the world

day filled with someone cats on the roof small case

butterflies arriving on same plane June 4 take care

shadowed gray line of cloud above shoulder of ridge

white line of wave breaking on sand next to channel

12.27

light coming into blue whiteness of sky above ridge

shadowed bamboo leaves moving in wind next to fence

nature of which place in the idea of action appears

present fact of particular area when applied toward

silhouette of crow calling from tip of black branch

white line of jet trail in blue white sky behind it

reddish orange of sky above black shoulder of ridge

shadowed white lines of waves breaking into channel

12.28

cloudless blue white sky above black plane of ridge

sparrows pecking up seeds from feeder next to fence

another holds the beginning caught up in reflection

more than form the mixture of sadness most personal

mother recalling finding best friend in living room

seated at 12-foot grand piano playing her heart out

blinding whiteness of sun next to shoulder of ridge

shadowed swell lines moving toward mouth of channel

12.29

light gray rain cloud against still invisible ridge

line of sparrows standing on edge of shadowed fence

situation somewhat follows physical concept of time

point belonging to direction of the line tangent to

parallel lines of light green edges of road on left

shadow on road to the right slanting toward horizon

gray white rain cloud against invisible top of ridge

shadowed lines of waves approaching mouth of channel

12.30

cloudless blue white sky above black plane of ridge

shadowed shape of bamboo leaf next to redwood fence

landscape view until the fall was said to have gone

arms crossed likewise the right leg picture drawing

under the surface is the presence of something else

walking around breathing seeing trees hearing birds

reddish orange of sky above black shoulder of ridge

shadowed swell lines moving toward mouth of channel

12.31

line of cloud in blue blackness of sky beside ridge

shadowed bird landing on edge of fence above feeder

position turn to effect of sight and color of scene

rather arrives in such a way that future is present

bird one sees out the upstairs bedroom window these

words perched on the branch witness to its presence

reddish orange of sky above black shoulder of ridge

shadowed line of swell approaching mouth of channel

1.1

light gray whiteness of clouds above shadowed ridge

sparrows pecking up seeds from bricks next to fence

place in the world can pass from nothing which here

follow one toward variant form of potential passage

one on right whose right index finger bends surgeon

one on left wearing aviator glasses sweater his son

sun comes up through clouds above shoulder of ridge

shadowed white lines of waves breaking into channel

1.2

light in window opposite unmade yellow and blue bed

patterns of leaves on branches moving on white wall

evening coming home works with much of this obvious

over what was once that could be more than presence

thinking about looking at landscape from a distance

light in the room through the window made of shapes

what circle of sun in cloud above shoulder of ridge

shadowed line of swell approaching mouth of channel

1.3

white lines of clouds in pale blue sky beside ridge

blue jay landing on edge of redwood fence by feeder

as light follows relations between different places

line the length of then in the direction of present

missing a bird or two the way the line makes a grid

two sets of three telephone wires in blue white sky

yellow red orange of clouds above shoulder of ridge

white line of wave breaking across mouth of channel

1.4

curved edge of cloud in pale blue sky next to ridge

two sparrows perched on feeder beside redwood fence

landscape as demonstration held before actual event

picture the same day simplified legs uncrossed feet

left then right foot walking through pools on trail

reflection of cloud branches overhead pace of sound

pinkish edges of gray cloud above shoulder of ridge

shadowed swell lines moving toward mouth of channel

1.5

cloudless pale blue sky beside black plane of ridge

orange of sun rising through shadowed bamboo leaves

light under star-filled sky letter a few days since

arrival of word happens as present which is to come

hand glancing back to being grasped as act grounded

present all the way back to the idea of speaking it

blinding whiteness of sun next to shoulder of ridge

parallel swell lines moving toward mouth of channel

1.6

light comes into pale blue sky above plane of ridge

red orange edge of sun in bamboo leaves above fence

possibly find its way into words followed by effect

evident from tone passage against the end of seeing

say the same thing twice opposite of making it this

more than where the subject could be made "subject"

blinding whiteness of sun next to shoulder of ridge

vertical yellow line of light in motionless channel

1.7

light pink line of cloud above black plane of ridge

shadowed bird flapping toward edge of redwood fence

think of trying to bring into focus something there

material close to the phrase makes it repeat shadow

remembering diagonal shaft of light slanting across

invisible ridge yellow of sun on surface of channel

blinding white edge of sun on horizon next to ridge

shadowed line of swell approaching mouth of channel

1.8

faint pink of cloud moving to the right above ridge

shadowed sparrows standing on edge of redwood fence

material kind of speaking somewhat first as follows

potential of field at point here description we see

first lines looking at what I see and hear going on

out there ridge below sky "I" become an ear and eye

blinding white circle of sun comes up next to ridge

shadowed swell lines moving toward mouth of channel

1.9

rain cloud moving to the right above shadowed ridge

white-crowned sparrow landing on feeder below fence

seen the movement made evening held in order to see

somewhat left but still responsive portion of dream

likewise the last two lines some kind of mesmerizes

attention to whatever being looked at minute shifts

dark gray rain cloud against invisible top of ridge

shadowed white wave breaking into windblown channel

1.10

white line of cloud in blue white sky next to ridge

sun coming up in shadowed bamboo leaves above fence

letter will continue a new picture of outside night

present saying the time on that day in such a shape

emotional feeling in response to this can't explain

see same thing each day moon comes up sun goes down

yellow red orange of sky by black shoulder of ridge

parallel swell lines moving toward mouth of channel

1.11

diagonal edge of cloud in pale blue sky above ridge

seven sparrows standing on fence across from feeder

near the idea of an intention would be able to swim

structure refers to number of conditions final line

first words in the first four scenes of Shakespeare

Twelfth Night makes an ABBA If What What If pattern

blinding whiteness of sun below cloud next to ridge

yellow line of light floating on motionless channel

1.12

pink light coming into clouds beside shadowed ridge

black shapes of bamboo leaves next to redwood fence

closer to what is closest now to be nearer at first

as for landscape setting the last hour of the night

seen from view which changes as soon as it is named

knowledge that transposes itself into simple action

yellow red orange sky above black shoulder of ridge

white lines of waves breaking into mouth of channel

1.13

cloudless blue white sky above black plane of ridge

two sparrows perched on redwood fence beside feeder

two events taking place simultaneous appear instant

field relative to time of describing certain action

writing down exactly what happens in moment of real

actual perception of sound as acoustic shape in air

blinding white edge of sun on horizon next to ridge

white line of light reflected in motionless channel

1.14

diagonal lines of white clouds above plane of ridge

line of sparrows standing on edge of shadowed fence

same painting a lasting one also seems at this time

dream armature of planes think form and containment

something conditioned outside what is to be thought

less than thinking in the sense of made things seen

whiteness of sun coming up behind cloud above ridge

two cormorants flapping to the right toward horizon

1.15

pink cloud in pale blue sky above still black ridge

whiteness of waning moon next to tip of rose branch

there figures of people light on house and sidewalk

way by which what it is doing keeps at once present

man standing in blue pajamas woman in black sitting

faces him window between them blue chair blue walls

yellow red orange sky above black shoulder of ridge

shadowed swell lines moving toward mouth of channel

1.16

rain clouds moving against invisible plane of ridge

windblown black pine branches next to redwood fence

actual same experience of idea which something sees

rather than the second material approach to subject

relation between one's experience in actual present

world and words transcribed on two-dimensional page

gray rain cloud against invisible shoulder of ridge

whiteness of wave breaking across windblown channel

1.17

diagonal pink line of cloud above still black ridge

sparrows standing on edge of shadowed redwood fence

closest therefore to the seeing of sense perception

before morning part the story of light in sky seems

atmosphere on other side of someone who sees action

intersection changed by what appears to be going on

reddish edge of gray cloud beside shoulder of ridge

moon in pale blue sky above NO PARKING ANYTIME sign

1.18

gray lines of clouds in blue white sky beside ridge

towhees on bricks across from green glass back door

observe from the point interval at rest relative to

describe another moving point passing through world

something about perception of things out the window

seen and heard in words that change that site scene

blinding whiteness of sun above cloud next to ridge

white line of light reflected on motionless channel

1.19

gray whiteness of clouds above shadowed green ridge

motion of green bamboo leaves next to redwood fence

light surrounding solid volumes what they saw heard

both become less the limit of doors overhead floats

fact of attention to word enactment events in world

happens when one stops to see hears it taking place

red orange of cloud next to black shoulder of ridge

white lines of waves breaking into mouth of channel

1.20

light in window opposite unmade yellow and blue bed

birds line up on edge of redwood fence above feeder

brightness of streets pinkish violet front of house

what occurs gathers which has passed away before it

one continues to think in retrospect about painting

murals on bottom of swimming pool filled with water

gray whiteness of sky above black shoulder of ridge

diagonal white line of wave breaking across channel

1.21

light gray rain cloud against still invisible ridge

sparrows lined up on edge of shadowed redwood fence

see at least for a moment situation comes into play

method a fact objective mention sun as much as wind

moving between action we can't see to action we can

whose exterior surface reflects that interior action

gray white rain cloud above black shoulder of ridge

windblown white wave breaking into mouth of channel

1.22

triangular gray cloud in blue white sky above ridge

5 white-crowned sparrows lining up on redwood fence

look what holds under visible things between vision

so often by 10 o'clock the difference between seems

looks like shadowed tree at lowest point of horizon

field of grass below sunlit clouds in pale blue sky

white edge of sun coming up above clouds on horizon

white line of wave breaking across mouth of channel

1.23

dream in unmade yellow and blue bed opposite window

photograph of father still looking like Johnny Cash

same time holds simultaneous light in higher degree

point as before the center of curvature normal line

eyes drifting across the page finding certain words

opposite to how everything changes someone on paper

yellow red orange sky above black shoulder of ridge

shadowed line of swell approaching mouth of channel

1.24

light coming into clouds above black plane of ridge

blue jay landing on edge redwood fence above feeder

lasting one was also present seems open before that

over as shaded light seeing symbol of the sun's eye

located in place things and events in which looking

move between window closing and reflection in glass

pale orange of clouds above black shoulder of ridge

line of shadowed swell approaching mouth of channel

1.25

gray blackness of sky against still invisible ridge

motionless black pine branches beside redwood fence

street under a blue sky stars dark violet and green

passed the once present partake in what is presumed

speaking of no sound the first one that comes along

change from making to whatever comes of consequence

gray line of light on horizon to the right of ridge

sound of waves breaking on sand across from channel

1.26

white edge of gray cloud above shadowed green ridge

two white-crowned sparrows landing on redwood fence

chosen because this way knows the following instant

person not possible to refer to the sun wind viewed

what was happening in the picture an event material

person's hand approaching the two-dimensional plane

sunlit whiteness of cloud next to shoulder of ridge

shadowed line of swell approaching mouth of channel

1.27

gray whiteness of fog against still invisible ridge

white-crowned sparrow landing on fence above feeder

overlook through which seeing hurries to experience

in between the next few lines either future or past

arrangement of letters in words running across page

think of lines as enactments of how and what we see

gray whiteness of fog still against invisible ridge

white lines of waves breaking into mouth of channel

1.28

light gray rain cloud against still invisible ridge

two towhees pecking up seeds on bricks below feeder

from any other which could be from these particular

straight line imagined parallel to a starting point

sound as an acoustic shape its shape a visual sound

each line separate and connected to lines around it

gray white rain cloud still against invisible ridge

sound of white water breaking into mouth of channel

1.29

blue white of sky above sunlit green slope of ridge

sun rising into windblown bamboo leaves above fence

before opened a one-day appearance still figurative

panels of sun shadows light the existence of planes

shapes of clouds following sun line on moving water

listener hearing sound of waves breaking in channel

blinding white circle of sun in clouds beside ridge

yellow line of light reflected in windblown channel

1.30

light in window opposite unmade yellow and blue bed

golden-crowned sparrow beside green glass back door

tree a night picture black beautiful blue and green

suspend in duration less now bound in world's night

glare of water breaking on rocks in black and white

pair of photos left one with body the other without

gray whiteness of fog against still invisible ridge

white line of wave breaking on sand next to channel

1.31

pale orange lines of clouds above still black ridge

motionless green bamboo leaves beside redwood fence

following something should have been done from what

people finding what there was of it after so-called

moving from looking at asking what happened to each

present moment takes place here and everywhere else

yellow red orange of clouds above shoulder of ridge

shadowed line of swell approaching mouth of channel

2.1

cloudless blue white sky above shadowed green ridge

blue jay landing on edge of redwood fence by feeder

seeing passed over as easiest because most familiar

there transforms into the step that is exactly fact

transition from most will come to occur in thinking

everything where and when events nothing other than

blinding white circle of sun next to shadowed ridge

white line of light reflected in motionless channel

2.2

diagonal white lines of clouds above shadowed ridge

quails pecking up seeds on edge of bricks by feeder

space and time in relation therefore asking whether

imagine system of reference follows direction where

namely now since no matter whether perceived or not

how those who know part ones who want to be touched

blinding white circle of sun in clouds beside ridge

white lines of waves breaking into mouth of channel

2.3

cloudless blue white sky above black plane of ridge

motion of shadowed green bamboo leaves beside fence

themselves in certain still recovering from evening

figures like themselves space with shadowed surface

night picture a tree black beautiful blue and green

suspending duration now bound less in world's night

yellow red orange sky above black shoulder of ridge

shadowed swell lines moving toward mouth of channel

2.4

high thin white clouds in pale blue sky above ridge

white-crowned sparrow landing on fence above feeder

done with nothing but yellow color night in picture

what remains in this building thinking what follows

thinking of speech still naming the ability to hear

history whose events are nothing say by saying that

blinding whiteness of sun next to still black ridge

parallel swell lines moving toward mouth of channel

2.5

horizontal line of shadowed gray cloud beside ridge

sparrow slanting from corner of fence toward feeder

immediate instant taken action once begun something

line of functions like the first noted demonstrates

between the fact that sets itself off and the other

hand grounded in that view of thinking of something

red orange lines of clouds beside shoulder of ridge

diagonal line of swell approaching mouth of channel

2.6

light coming into cloudless blue black sky by ridge

motionless black pine branches beside redwood fence

think about what is least thought see what is close

evening condition of light function of scene itself

cypress tree with sun behind it just at this moment

thinking one sees what's there before it disappears

pale red orange edge of sky above shoulder of ridge

swell lines moving across nearly motionless channel

2.7

light coming into fog against still invisible ridge

shadowed sparrow slanting to the right toward fence

as well as asking what passes from one to the other

direction defined first moving on second takes form

between one and another consequence visible so that

present depicted as what is most present itself one

pale red orange sky above line of fog against ridge

white line of wave breaking on sand next to channel

2.8

cloudless pale blue sky above sunlit green of ridge

two sparrows standing on edge of fence above feeder

saw aspects in the view which included list of part

shadows in the glare of the eye understood as point

looking out from where you stand looking at me what

do you see sunlight on the hill piano as background

blinding white circle of sun coming up beside ridge

motion of light reflected in windblown blue channel

2.9

cloudless blue white sky above black plane of ridge

motion of shadowed green bamboo leaves across fence

day after the sketch things in the dark may mistake

thinking about building discover view of that place

thinking say by saying this event is this fact that

transition the reference to experience of seeing it

blinding whiteness of sun next to shoulder of ridge

white lines of waves breaking into mouth of channel

2.10

bright blue whiteness of sky next to shadowed ridge

streaked sparrow flapping toward feeder below fence

here it was who held view implies notion of instant

reading source relates to some found in translation

looking down at diagonal black line of the sandspit

color gone out of the world after the sun goes down

blinding white circle of sun comes up next to ridge

line of light reflected in still motionless channel

2.11

light in window opposite unmade yellow and blue bed

whiteness of planet next to pine branch above fence

closest experience follows from ground of beginning

atmosphere of feeling landscape image in foreground

interior of room projected onto landscape in window

horizontal green field next to shadowed green ridge

yellow red orange edge of sky to the right of ridge

white circle of moon beside NO PARKING ANYTIME sign

2.12

gray line of fog against light blue sky above ridge

whiteness of waning moon next to tip of rose branch

moving relative to it maybe shown by means of light

stand in circumstance compare action of one another

two figures facing opposite abyss of window opening

into the garden narrative driving across long lines

left edge of fog against shadowed shoulder of ridge

moon beside right corner of NO PARKING ANYTIME sign

2.13

light comes into fog against invisible top of ridge

blue jay standing on edge of shadowed redwood fence

continued present second called landscape of fields

multiple spatial lines moving in intersecting lines

line breaks making visual shape of the right margin

things action events going on from moment to moment

gray whiteness of fog against top of shadowed ridge

shadowed swell lines moving toward mouth of channel

2.14

light coming into blue blackness of fog above ridge

shadowed towhee flapping from edge of redwood fence

take blue or green way of conventional night scenes

idea building in which everything that is in place

looking down at shadowed black line of the sandspit

color gone out of the world after the sun goes down

gray whiteness of fog above black shoulder of ridge

swell line approaching otherwise motionless channel

2.15

sunlit white clouds next to shadowed green of ridge

motion of sparrow flapping from feeder toward fence

instant at which one is transferred to another time

letter to those days how difficult it was sometimes

slightly east of you under cloudless pale blue late

afternoon skies in perfect storm of missed messages

blinding white circle of sun next to shadowed ridge

white line of light reflected in motionless channel

2.16

white clouds in light blue sky next to sunlit ridge

red finches perched on feeder next to redwood fence

see beginning at first to show itself there appears

foreground much as later negative part of landscape

something between one and another visible confusion

present depicted as what is being in relation to it

white circle of sun rising into clouds beside ridge

swell lines approaching motionless mouth of channel

2.17

blue white sky beside tree-lined green top of ridge

white-crowned sparrow on feeder below redwood fence

think space time physical from one point to another

where relation to velocity along in four dimensions

pink red edge of blue blackness of cloud in picture

somehow looking like painting stopped motion effect

blinding whiteness of sun next to shoulder of ridge

shadowed swell lines moving toward mouth of channel

2.18

lines of gray clouds in blue black sky next to ridge

white edge of waning moon in shadowed green branches

continuing to divide attention returned home to see

direction for door somewhere converges with another

rose an experience changes in that sense looking at

how sounds of words in line register things outside

orange of sky beside clouds above shoulder of ridge

white curve of moon next to NO PARKING ANYTIME sign

2.19

cloudless blue edge of sky beside still black ridge

upturned curve of waning moon next to bamboo branch

whitish light where yellows and orange told whether

only these buildings limit at home on the way there

whether something springs from the question it asks

first in other words whether thinking belongs to it

orange of sky next to still black shoulder of ridge

shadowed swell lines moving toward mouth of channel

2.20

diagonal line of cloud in pale blue sky above ridge

edge of sun in shadowed bamboo leaves next to fence

each of two pieces said instants which is continual

thought then adding sometimes in those days subject

not to say something springs from question it asked

decides in other words first thinking belongs to it

whiteness of sun in cloud next to shoulder of ridge

line of white light reflected in motionless channel

2.21

diagonal white cloud in blue white sky beside ridge

silhouette of crow on black pine branch above fence

inward beginning even there can still remain veiled

later exterior what would call the passage in lines

knowing how to put a preposition at end of the line

whether or not to register line breaks reading them

blinding white circle of sun comes up next to ridge

shadowed line of swell approaching mouth of channel

2.22

light coming into blue blackness of sky above ridge

planet below cloud by shadowed branch next to fence

measured distance between two points of light place

action of moving point another in relation to space

speaking about how vowel tones lead the rhythm what

was actually happening there on the stage of a page

gray blue sky between lines of clouds next to ridge

shadowed white lines of waves breaking into channel

2.23

gray line of light in blackness of sky beside ridge

sound of wind moving in bamboo branches above fence

way to see still made also on the page saw painting

intersect set of points dispersed indoor space lane

something comes out of perception of things happens

relations between things pulling together and apart

blackness of sky next to still black plane of ridge

orange line of light on horizon across from channel

2.24

cloudless blue of sky beside tree-lined green ridge

motion of shadowed green bamboo leaves across fence

what you think of now beginning to be a description

dwelling place here a home house to take shelter in

even if now after naming different time in anything

now that it will be taken as some objective present

white circle of sun in bright blue sky beside ridge

white line of light reflected in motionless channel

2.25

clcudless blue white sky next to sunlit green ridge

white-crowned sparrow landing on tip of rose branch

see to begin would be taken up somewhere to move it

not the object first to be sure the question of say

thinking on the one hand related to asking question

name for the line horizon in which such become both

blinding yellow whiteness of sun rising above ridge

white line of wave breaking across mouth of channel

2.26

pale blue whiteness of sky beside still black ridge

sound of song sparrow calling from right foreground

here beginning first itself what has come behind it

ends with image of hands grass in touch with nature

shape of words in song as rhythm and sound patterns

coupled with melodic and rhythmic patterns of notes

first edge of sun coming up above shoulder of ridge

swell lines moving across nearly motionless channel

2.27

blue white edge of sky next to still shadowed ridge

motionless green bamboo leaves beside redwood fence

velocity of light relative to what may be motion of

three dimensional space reformed between disappears

do not think I'm not here spare time thinking about

two detachable identities one in words one in music

blinding white circle of sun coming up beside ridge

line of light reflected in still motionless channel

2.28

light coming into lines of clouds above black ridge

bird flapping to the right from feeder toward fence

form of attention most in those capable of grasping

lines of sight crossing space depths a linear event

pattern of a song's music completed every two lines

unit of line overlapped by a unit of musical phrase

yellow red orange of clouds above shoulder of ridge

white line of wave breaking on sand next to channel

2.29

light in window opposite unmade yellow and blue bed

shadowed bamboo leaves moving next to redwood fence

think of starlit night approximate the same subject

today even this much house may even be easy to keep

four days before mother's birthday someone arriving

home walking up path with cat her face in her hands

blinding white circle of sun in clouds beside ridge

line of white wave breaking on sand next to channel

3.1

sunlit white clouds in blue white sky next to ridge

shadowed bird perched on redwood fence above feeder

somewhere less open situation capable of background

important but the fact is to be changed in a letter

different kinds of rhyme like relationships between

certain words "cat" "rat" "cat" "mouse" "cat" "dog"

white circle of sun next to black shoulder of ridge

white lines of waves breaking on sandbar in channel

3.2

cloudless blue white sky above black plane of ridge

blue jay moves from edge of redwood fence to feeder

beginning in that way here an experience of what is

face as much as the boy in one reading of sentiment

syllables and notes both having duration takes time

attachment of rhythmic texture to tones feeling too

pale red orange sky next to black shoulder of ridge

shadowed line of swell approaching mouth of channel

3.3

cloudless pale blue white sky beside shadowed ridge

song sparrow calling from rose branch in foreground

constancy of light may be the principle of velocity

between attraction when two points of mass describe

complex simplicity inherent in music + words + song

two parts pulling simultaneously together and apart

blinding white circle of sun next to shadowed ridge

line of white light reflected in motionless channel

3.4

high thin white clouds in pale blue sky above ridge

blue jay flapping from shadowed fence toward feeder

paintings of earliest objects appear which elements

counterpoint of optical idea enfolds inside instant

another order in the disorder its absence now shows

sounds unfolding moment by moment in listener's ear

white circle of sun coming up in clouds above ridge

yellow line of light reflection in windless channel

3.5

gray white clouds beside still black plane of ridge

3 sparrows standing on redwood fence next to feeder

just the yellow house on paper signed end of letter

shelters open to air light and sun dwelling in them

now yel- echoed in the reverse assonance of let now

el sound in first syllable of yellow echoed in well

gray white of clouds against invisible top of ridge

white line of wave breaking on sand next to channel

3.6

gray whiteness of clouds above still shadowed ridge

blue jay flapping from fence to bricks below feeder

transform experience of a sort time to time suppose

change identified as memory of object in this light

1 unit each for "time" "speech" "all" "some" "some"

"Summer" "Winter" less expansive than these actions

low light gray clouds above black shoulder of ridge

shadowed line of swell approaching mouth of channel

3.7

light gray rain cloud against still invisible ridge

drops falling on wet red bricks below redwood fence

possibility of thinking the beginning to everything

even reading the balance between inward and outward

not the presence of any one pattern but the density

so many different interrelated patterns overlapping

gray of rain clouds against black shoulder of ridge

white lines of waves breaking into mouth of channel

3.8

white line of cloud in bright blue sky beside ridge

red-shouldered hawk calling on branch in foreground

light therefore consistent which transforms effects

lines exactly the same as that given now take place

arrangement of letters in syllables words and lines

shape place and time of day on two-dimensional page

blinding white circle of sun in cloud next to ridge

white line of light reflected in motionless channel

3.9

sunlit white cloud in bright blue sky next to ridge

shadowed sparrow flapping from fence to rose branch

elements of vocabulary simple bottle on a table top

spaces in the still life house these simultaneities

now sound echoed in hours clouds towers now and now

vowel-plus-n pattern in winter is echoed in enlarge

oval-shaped white of sun above clouds next to ridge

sunlit whiteness of swell lines in mouth of channel

3.10

white line of cloud in bright blue sky beside ridge

line of birds on edge of redwood fence above feeder

private letter sent by son a part of his collection

places in turn remain determined by insofar as that

right margin makes the visual shape slanting across

to the left each letter occupies same width on page

white circle of sun rising into clouds beside ridge

line of white wave breaking on sand next to channel

3.11

sunlit and shadowed whiteness of clouds above ridge

sparrow slanting across edge of fence toward feeder

room to move in the sentence play on the word field

view suggested color the exceptional nature of work

pattern of an opening outdoor winter scene movement

to chimneys blazing cups filled with wine and words

white circle of sun beside clouds across from ridge

shadowed swell lines moving toward mouth of channel

3.12

gray whiteness of fog against still invisible ridge

shadowed towhee pecking up seed from edge of bricks

still the beginning simultaneous in that way begins

special to pin down evening gathering ready to read

reader who senses operation of an unknown principle

order of symmetry and proportion its presence shows

gray whiteness of fog still against invisible ridge

sound of waves breaking on sand across from channel

3.13

gray whiteness of clouds above shadowed green ridge

two towhees on bricks next to green glass back door

this before these forms in detail of space and time

consider the case where zero is to be taken at rest

composer who spells out length of each musical note

pianist who knows exactly how long to hold down key

gray whiteness of clouds by black shoulder of ridge

whiteness of wave breaking across windblown channel

3.14

gray rain cloud against top of shadowed green ridge

towhee standing on grape stake fence by green field

surface which nearly parallel to picture plane form

imagining the answer always both here and elsewhere

words as action which actors speaking words perform

where they come from where they go into air and ear

grays of rain clouds beside black shoulder of ridge

white line of wave breaking on sand next to channel

3.15

light coming into gray rain cloud above black ridge

first bird chirping from branch in right foreground

at least perhaps between descent to private present

sides related end and means as long as this in mind

whole made of parts in relationships to one another

now winter nights enlarge the number of their hours

sunlit and shadowed clouds beside shoulder of ridge

line of white wave breaking on sand next to channel

3.16

light gray rain cloud above shadowed green of ridge

silhouettes of 3 sparrows standing on edge of fence

something to hold it away from object it means that

even water signed and dated color connected to here

transition the way the future takes over first time

become means to rise out of there remain occurrence

gray white rain cloud across from shoulder of ridge

diagonal white line of wave breaking across channel

3.17

white line of fog above top of shadowed green ridge

blinding circle of sun in bamboo leaves above fence

conceals what comes to pass at the end of the story

wants the light abstracted conversation sympathetic

clouds storms charge inviting same speech intensity

middle of line slightly more weighted down than end

sun rising into cloud across from shoulder of ridge

lines of white waves breaking into mouth of channel

3.18

gray rain cloud above shadowed green plane of ridge

towhee standing on grape stake fence across from it

make remarks about time separate space of reference

move under the force which given in the place which

syllables and notes matters of duration taking time

attachment of rhythmic texture to tones feeling too

light gray rain cloud above black shoulder of ridge

shadowed swell line moving across windblown channel

3.19

sunlit and shadowed gray white clouds next to ridge

two towhees pecking up seeds on bricks below feeder

bottle with jabs of paint reduced to geometric form

presence looks at world vision sight which can roam

metrically stressed syllables in masks court sights

stressed by downbeat sights also emphasized by time

sunlit edges of cloud across from shoulder of ridge

shadowed swell lines moving toward mouth of channel

3.20

line of white cloud in blue white sky next to ridge

crow standing on edge of redwood fence above feeder

additional observations after eighty years of place

how this is all that something in view of relations

however reflection thinking the line leads to sight

something in the direction of object makes it known

blinding whiteness of sun next to shoulder of ridge

line of light reflected in blue of channel below it

3.21

horizontal gray line of cloud beside plane of ridge

silhouettes of 7 sparrows lined up on edge of fence

there for it possibilities which tend to be observe

color originally itself another called the red spot

especially when one can't tell when black and white

photograph of clouds and water in color become tone

white circle of sun in gray white cloud above ridge

parallel swell lines moving toward mouth of channel

3.22

horizontal white cloud in pale blue sky above ridge

wind moving through green bamboo leaves above fence

completion of the story which later includes future

melancholy furthest to the left who is doing simply

sound of birds make birds seem like parts of plants

motion of rose moving in breeze breath leaving body

sunlit white edges of cloud above shoulder of ridge

white lines of waves breaking into mouth of channel

3.23

white edge of sun in clouds above still black ridge

motion of shadowed green bamboo leaves across fence

two simultaneous events happened as instant of time

first place equal to will be seen positions in time

in hearing a song one hears the words twice at once

as they sound and as they would sound without music

shaft of sun slanting down from clouds beside ridge

parallel swell lines breaking into mouth of channel

3.24

gray rain cloud above shadowed green plane of ridge

sound of first birds calling in field in foreground

two rectangles seeming objects sensation of density

physiological embrace return of aspect from the eye

rose in the distance positioned between V of petals

above sunlit larger rose's open mouth in foreground

light gray rain cloud above black shoulder of ridge

white wave breaking into windblown mouth of channel

3.25

blinding white circle of sun by cloud next to ridge

motion of shadowed green bamboo leaves across fence

graphic correspondence understood featured in light

view of means way toward dwelling who tells us this

lengthening of metrically stressed syllables in now

yellow waxen lights set to sequence of longer notes

whiteness of sun in cloud next to shoulder of ridge

line of white light reflected in motionless channel

3.26

dream in unmade yellow and blue bed opposite window

friend comes back from the dead wears black wetsuit

dream of real imagination of there is nothing to do

item connected to composition two colors related to

perception of feeling with no less than the feeling

wonder what moving under a breaking wave feels like

blinding white circle of sun coming up beside ridge

white lines of waves breaking into mouth of channel

3.27

cloudless pale blue sky beside shadowed green ridge

motion of green bamboo leaves on branch above fence

follow the beginning even therefore what is closest

waiting for the next letter speak different effects

speech stresses at end of the line well-tun'd words

an increase of duration from well to tun'd to words

blinding white circle of sun by cloud next to ridge

sunlit line of wave breaking into windblown channel

3.28

motionless light gray clouds against green of ridge

rufous-sided towhee on edge of fence next to feeder

point of space observe event of something happening

moving on the second now here three relations where

motion of rose bud against end of cut cypress trunk

blows in wind less like a plant more like an animal

gray of rain cloud above shadowed shoulder of ridge

white line of wave breaking across mouth of channel

3.29

light gray rain cloud against still invisible ridge

3 sparrows lined up on redwood fence next to feeder

sensation rather than line closer to him than those

physical amplified by seeing what used to be called

sound of crow calling brings black into the picture

pink rose in mind's eye someone else might see bird

gray white rain cloud above black shoulder of ridge

sunlit curve of wave breaking into mouth of channel

3.30

sunlit whiteness of cloud next to still black ridge

towhee pecking up seed on brick below redwood fence

respond to document about apparently writing letter

take measure of building tell about nature of thing

what it means to write one each day almost the same

inscribed in the landscape as if another part of it

light and darker gray cloud above shoulder of ridge

line of white wave breaking across mouth of channel

3.31

gray whiteness of fog against still invisible ridge

rufous-sided towhee standing on bricks below feeder

no sooner taken than being there nothing as long as

position received back from the first page of color

fan-shaped yellow of sunlight below dark gray cloud

breaking into sky red orange horizon heart in mouth

horizontal plane of cloud against shoulder of ridge

white line of wave breaking on sand next to channel

4.1

blinding white edge of sun beside still black ridge

blue jay standing on edge of shadowed redwood fence

overlook a lack of attention sequence of experience

breaks the letter not for long word turning to none

two words in same position of two consecutive lines

placement of one- and two-syllable words every line

white circle of sun in bright blue sky beside ridge

line of white wave breaking across mouth of channel

4.2

sun coming up into cloudless blue sky next to ridge

blue jay pecking at seed on edge of fence by feeder

element of continuum obscured the character of time

moving now takes the form of relative to one stands

now at beginning of line 1 set to same note as time

well and first syllable of leaden sounded in spells

white circle of sun in bright blue sky beside ridge

line of white wave breaking across mouth of channel

4.3

horizontal white cloud in pale blue sky above ridge

wind moving through bamboo leaves across from fence

exposure to methods seems approach to breaking down

sees from elsewhere at the same time person in whom

invisible birds calling in rose bush next to bricks

bird sounds appearing below clouds in pale blue sky

blinding white circle of sun in clouds beside ridge

white line of wave breaking to the right of channel

4.4

gray white rain cloud against still invisible ridge

sound of birds calling in green field in foreground

back of sketch of yellow house final page of letter

meantime talk of spoken words shape in fact perhaps

words different from those same words sung to music

whose four long beats of tonic resolution on nights

light gray rain cloud still against invisible ridge

shadowed line of swell approaching mouth of channel

4.5

light gray rain cloud still against invisible ridge

hummingbird standing on shadowed tip of rose branch

only to act itself can see the field of possibility

received at first in other words two works together

first one metrically unstressed the second stressed

evenness of penultimate line's quarter-note setting

gray white rain cloud against top of shadowed ridge

parallel swell lines moving toward mouth of channel

4.6

white edge of sun below cloud beside shadowed ridge

blue jay landing on apple tree branch next to fence

extreme between woman in painting done years before

still the look of beginning what is close expressed

thinking of maiden moaning to climb south hill pick

jagged fern see no man who shall not pine and yearn

shaft of sunlight slanting down from cloud by ridge

shadowed line of swell approaching mouth of channel

4.7

sunlit edge of cloud in bright blue sky above ridge

blue jay cracking seeds on table across from feeder

conception of time particular simultaneity of space

circumstance when previous action of moving another

were that you would visit me in this gray wet world

hole in the convertible roof where the rain gets in

sun behind cloud in pale blue sky across from ridge

shadowed swell lines moving toward mouth of channel

4.8

gray white of clouds against invisible top of ridge

sound of bird chirping on branch in left foreground

reconstructing dissolved forms refractions of light

being the counterpart of a body which is everywhere

someone saying he isn't much yet but has good stuff

everyone in fluid becoming whose beings are in flux

light gray of clouds against invisible top of ridge

diagonal white line of wave breaking across channel

4.9

edges of cloud moving to the left above green ridge

red-shouldered hawk calling on branch in foreground

sketch described as illustration belonging to paper

version that drives nature into means of expression

tendency for persons to turn inward upon themselves

response to loss of all expression of one's emotion

horizontal gray plane of cloud by shoulder of ridge

parallel swell lines moving toward mouth of channel

4.10

sunlit edges of clouds above tree-lined green ridge

bird chirping in shadowed green field in foreground

see beneath these points as soon as suggest another

circle on third page of the house the rest of color

self-deception to look at stars wait for revelation

nature of child to believe he is center of universe

shadowed gray white clouds beside shoulder of ridge

parallel swell lines moving toward mouth of channel

4.11

gray whiteness of clouds against top of black ridge

sound of song sparrow calling from right foreground

first version of essay less than vision of thinking

something vaguely glimpse speaks of return of light

some poems and smoothly each sung to a quarter note

summer's first syllable set to pair of eighth notes

gray white plane of cloud against shoulder of ridge

diagonal white edge of wave breaking across channel

4.12

gray of cloud against top of tree-lined green ridge

bird flapping to the left from fence toward cypress

point or instant in time in which something happens

relation here in three dimensional space disappears

pale pink rose petal against diagonal cypress trunk

how turning sideways might change one's perspective

shaft of sunlight slanting down from cloud to ridge

white line of wave breaking on sand next to channel

4.13

sunlit edges of clouds in pale blue sky above ridge

sound of bird chirping in green field in foreground

surfaces of light behind which forms appear to turn

in body designed as potential to become one subject

one who eats flowers draws sun through moving lines

out from the cave away from fire moves toward ocean

blinding white circle of sun in clouds beside ridge

white line of wave breaking on sand next to channel

4.14

white edge of sun in cloudless blue sky above ridge

song sparrow calling from green field in foreground

note written at end of letter painted a description

part to be voiced everywhere means to stay in place

write what's happening in the actual present moment

speaking of the voice going forward in such measure

white circle of sun in bright blue sky beside ridge

line of light reflected in still motionless channel

4.15

blinding white circle of sun above tree-lined ridge

sunlit green of bamboo leaves next to redwood fence

between being silent in which case it could be said

enclosed triangle one red spot dated sometime after

begin to get somewhat a grasp on process of thought

how to express those feelings verbally or otherwise

sun in cloudless blue sky next to shoulder of ridge

white line of light reflected in motionless channel

4.16

light gray whiteness of clouds against top of ridge

motionless yellow of flower by bricks in foreground

idea of thinking about the world maybe too abstract

revealed connection between concealment and showing

no moon up there somewhere sun will show everything

duration of form clouds from one moment to the next

gray whiteness of clouds against top of black ridge

white line of wave breaking on sand next to channel

4.17

shadowed gray cloud against top of tree-lined ridge

song sparrow calling from branch in left foreground

physical event in space in reference between events

before the attraction toward when points take place

moving toward while simultaneously moving away from

as light going now moves away from day toward night

gray plane of cloud next to black shoulder of ridge

white line of wave breaking across mouth of channel

4.18

light gray of clouds next to tree-lined green ridge

song sparrow calling on edge of branch across fence

surfaces light behind which simplified forms repeat

body of self a matter of evidence from visual world

someone looking down on ocean as far as eye can see

another sees photo of red flower against green back

gray white clouds beside shadowed shoulder of ridge

diagonal white line of wave breaking across channel

4.19

plane of light gray clouds next to tree-lined ridge

blue jay flapping from redwood fence toward cypress

portrait painted of two errors proved only sentence

meaning verb namely lost preserved in word neighbor

never having talked with anyone about it no one has

talked with one about it takes place in these words

horizontal line of clouds in pale blue sky by ridge

diagonal line of wave breaking in middle of channel

4.20

gray of clouds beside tree-lined green top of ridge

hummingbird in motion next to green glass back door

glides over itself a conversion involving existence

after being separated many years from form has come

waves in the channel stirred up these last days one

swell after another south wind clouds against ridge

sunlit white line in clouds above shoulder of ridge

wingspan of pelican circling above mouth of channel

4.21

sun rising into clouds next to black plane of ridge

song sparrow calling from branch in left foreground

paragraph launched to set out form physical present

where revealed in connection between letting appear

thinking about here see relation to what follows is

where shape of the margin takes place in such lines

curve of white cloud in pale blue sky next to ridge

V-shaped line of 9 pelicans flapping toward channel

4.22

white edge of sun coming up above still black ridge

motion of yellow iris next to green glass back door

relations between events appear object in continuum

now in such a way taken as move which proceeds from

brick runway made one summer in the fog two planets

person going to disappear into the air without word

blinding whiteness of sun next to shoulder of ridge

white line of light reflected in motionless channel

4.23

blinding whiteness of sun next to still black ridge

motion of wind in sunlit yellow iris next to bricks

positions suggested impulse series of human figures

vision that falls from hand that sees resting in it

object following actions whether one sees it or not

state of time in which things witness to themselves

white circle of sun rising into clouds beside ridge

line of white light reflected in motionless channel

4.24

blinding circle of sun in cloudless bright blue sky

motion of sunlit yellow iris in wind next to bricks

postscript on back of sketch letter which described

neighbor in place of dwelling tells us how we think

one seeing two red fire trucks parked across street

another sitting with oxygen mask surrounded by EMTs

sun rising in cloudless bright blue sky above ridge

sunlit lines of swells approaching mouth of channel

4.25

sun coming up into cloud above still shadowed ridge

crow gliding to the left across field toward branch

how in this sentence play on field note presupposed

point of view in a letter after move into new house

one who sees another last time that moment eyes met

being helped down stairs in wheel chair after event

blinding white of sun above black shoulder of ridge

motion of white light reflected in mouth of channel

4.26

white circle of sun in bright blue sky beside ridge

unknown bird perched on shadowed post in foreground

form which connects future with past limits on hand

where in the light of day appearing between what is

how still there is to be about thought one had said

maybe the wrong thing becomes objects now forgotten

horizontal line of fog on horizon across from ridge

white of sun reflected in low tide mouth of channel

4.27

first white edge of sun rising above plane of ridge

motion of windblown tall green grasses across fence

two events appear sequel in three dimensional space

now given in the first place seen positions in time

day filled with things going on elsewhere over here

shadows of clouds on water wind strong as yesterday

white circle of sun next to black shoulder of ridge

silver of sunlight reflected on sand beside channel

4.28

white circle of sun in bright blue sky beside ridge

yellow of iris to the left of green glass back door

series of volumes repeated pattern crossing surface

simultaneity of aspects becomes a sense of physical

high thin white clouds through which waxing of moon

sound of frogs in otherwise blackness of 80 flowers

blinding whiteness of sun next to shoulder of ridge

horizontal line of fog moving into mouth of channel

4.29

white circle of sun in clouds beside green of ridge

sound of crows calling back and forth in foreground

seeing as letter after thought view perhaps to make

gives a clue to how we think when we speak of other

time to speak with him more clearly than was before

he never stopped working on things to do with water

white edge of sun in clouds above shoulder of ridge

line of white wave breaking on sand next to channel

4.30

white circle of sun next to cloud across from ridge

motion of tall green grasses in field next to fence

perception set out to ask whether in terms of which

opening cried out look here color happy to get back

walking along from here to there wind blown grasses

rock now in shadows how many years has it been here

whiteness of sun in clouds beside shoulder of ridge

shadowed swell lines moving toward mouth of channel

5.1

white circle of sun across from cloud next to ridge

hummingbird next to pink white flower in foreground

see as well as from this emerge concept of incident

appears in this way both the same and yet again not

moon still up there shining brightly did you see it

asleep on couch in red pajamas under a yellow quilt

blinding whiteness of sun next to shoulder of ridge

pelicans flapping to the left from point to channel

5.2

gray whiteness of fog against still invisible ridge

song sparrow calling from bamboo branch above fence

relation in space to object in nature at this point

except at times would take the place of may be seen

walking and talking and matches and view that shows

photographs and lines below windblown space outside

light gray whiteness of fog against invisible ridge

white line of wave breaking on sand next to channel

5.3

white circle of sun in bright blue sky beside ridge

crow flapping to edge of redwood fence above feeder

resemblance close to line of hills appears parallel

repeatable sense of focus vision which only expands

yellow of iris to the left of green glass back door

blackness of crows calling on branches we don't see

white circle of sun next to black shoulder of ridge

sunlit white lines of waves breaking across channel

5.4

blinding white circle of sun coming up beside ridge

hummingbird hovering to the left of glass back door

letter missing the last page going back to original

performs alongside here and there also says how far

shadows on paper appearing to be moving handwritten

page in relation to feel of typed gap between words

pale blue whiteness of sky beside shoulder of ridge

line of light reflected in still motionless channel

5.5

blinding white of sun beside tree-lined green ridge

grasses in field beginning to move as wind comes up

note previous aspect of thing made from proposition

color continues color remains after years of change

how notes in music change sounds of words in a song

rhythmic motion of words determined by song's notes

white circle of sun in blue white sky next to ridge

sunlit lines of waves approaching windblown channel

5.6

white circle of sun rising beside still black ridge

shadowed bamboo leaves moving next to redwood fence

how to mention attitude toward pictures and figures

same appearance in more than one way showing itself

one making late take off under breaking lip of wave

figure further inside disappearing into white water

blinding whiteness of sun next to shoulder of ridge

lines of waves breaking to the right across channel

5.7

blinding white circle of sun next to shadowed ridge

song sparrow calling on bamboo branch next to fence

fact of an event less in picture than form of touch

bodies also in world by any means in order to adapt

confined to a house place experience time as series

present moments rather than endless linear sequence

pale blue whiteness of sky beside shoulder of ridge

white line of wave breaking across mouth of channel

5.8

blinding white circle of sun coming up beside ridge

unseen birds chirping from field in left foreground

appears to believe knowing thinking might have seen

physical limit of form everything comes together in

father who feels pleasure in having son as shipmate

hoping to sail full many a league for years to come

blinding white sun by cloud above shoulder of ridge

white line of wave breaking on sand next to channel

5.9

gray whiteness of fog against top of shadowed ridge

silhouette of crow landing on edge of redwood fence

volume in lost last page different ending in letter

activity on the way to speaks in its original sense

listening to reading includes memory of that moment

someone talking about how the "d" turns into an "o"

gray white fog still against invisible top of ridge

diagonal white line of wave breaking across channel

5.10

gray whiteness of fog against top of shadowed ridge

unseen birds calling from branch across green field

position whether actual exchange nothing for anyone

water as water known when question is one of twelve

how turning sideways might change one's perspective

fading roses climbing over horizontal cypress trunk

gray white fog against still invisible top of ridge

line of white wave breaking across mouth of channel

5.11

light gray clouds moving right to left beside ridge

black wingspan of crow gliding into left foreground

rhythm of color kind of transparent line which time

light perceived as something appearance in sense of

bronze Buddha on granite rock in the window looking

out at ridge how the pause worked at the line break

whiteness of sun in clouds beside shoulder of ridge

white lines of wave breaking into windblown channel

5.12

light gray rain cloud against still invisible ridge

motionless wet green grasses in field in foreground

picturing relations in a visual continuum of events

like image of world which lies open to light of day

warm rain on roof at night rain soothing rain sound

rain here at least turning world into a green world

sunlit lower edge of clouds against invisible ridge

line of white wave breaking on sand next to channel

5.13

pale gray rain cloud against invisible top of ridge

sound of bird calling on branch in right foreground

contact with others which led to thinking of others

last of many figures with space makes both of these

one wakes from dream to one goes down to skate park

five minutes later breaks tibia fibula in right leg

gray white rain cloud against still invisible ridge

diagonal white line of wave breaking across channel

5.14

light gray rain cloud against still invisible ridge

2 streaked sparrows perched on feeder next to fence

found other page part of sketch of the yellow house

nature of dwelling which reaches in versions answer

too much emphasis on question of who you seem to be

wheels of life grind to a halt in search of answers

gray rain cloud against invisible shoulder of ridge

shadowed white wave breaking into windblown channel

5.15

white circle of sun rising next to tree-lined ridge

sound of crows calling from branches across from it

found in this one remains still idea find in things

memory then of date more than inscribed view letter

witness these things as calling of them and to them

one that is still calling even if it makes no sound

blinding whiteness sun in pale blue sky above ridge

line of white water breaking across sand in channel

5.16

sun rising into diagonal lines of cloud above ridge

2 blue jays standing on bricks beside redwood fence

color at the same time other moment at which moment

shining more and more relation to something counted

opening in clouds one star up there faint as a star

when one is shining in the sky otherwise sleep well

whiteness of sun in clouds beside still black ridge

line of pelicans gliding to the left toward channel

5.17

sun in light gray fog against still invisible ridge

quail on left corner of redwood fence in foreground

image of how space defined physical relations which

think of sequence even those who view between notes

sound of monosyllable sleeps in unstressed position

sequence of 5-note ascent from one line to the next

sunlight in fog against invisible shoulder of ridge

white line of wave breaking on sand next to channel

5.18

bright whiteness of sun beside clouds against ridge

swallow slanting toward edge of house in foreground

look with eye as well as one still was not the same

last series of forms third presences under one roof

vertical pale blue-framed window small rock on sill

looking at pink red rose flowers beginning to bloom

blinding white sun above cloud by shoulder of ridge

silver line of light reflected in windblown channel

5.19

blinding whiteness of sun above clouds beside ridge

yellow of iris next to pink red roses in foreground

page of letter found period how did it find its way

means to say at the same time sense making building

green surface of old growth boxwood geometry making

minimalist meaning to include the ideas it contains

sun rising into cloud above black shoulder of ridge

silver line of wave breaking into windblown channel

5.20

blinding whiteness of sun above cloud next to ridge

silhouette of crow landing on edge of redwood fence

position only as long as method thing without which

after memory in book blue stresses the circumstance

remembered dream going up to mesa too tired to walk

sound of kids riding along on bikes and skateboards

blinding white sun above cloud by shoulder of ridge

parallel blue lines of swells moving toward channel

5.21

edge of sun coming up above tree-lined top of ridge

sound of crows calling back and forth in foreground

isolation dissolved in words which reach to contain

something there in relation to subject modern sense

pattern of walnut tree branches below pale blue sky

whiteness of sun by man in black wetsuit's shoulder

white edge of sun in cloud beside shoulder of ridge

line of pelicans flapping from channel toward point

5.22

sun rising into cloudless pale blue sky above ridge

motion of sunlit grasses bending in windblown field

physical relations which show further time opposite

mental image of world which will be following given

man in white van seeing how waves middle of channel

went from beautiful novel to horror show in minutes

blinding white of sun in cloudless sky beside ridge

wingspan of osprey circling across mouth of channel

5.23

sun rising into cloudless pale blue sky above ridge

sound of unseen bird calling in field in foreground

one who for years had been combine idea of position

simultaneity of figure present the subject may seem

after all those weeks of rain the world around here

now appears to be covered over in light green paint

blinding circle of sun in pale blue sky above ridge

edge of triangular white wave breaking into channel

5.24

sun in high thin white clouds beside shadowed ridge

silhouette of sparrow on left edge of redwood fence

how the record appeared possibly also place between

sense of hand at first sight event more than change

opportunities for change in the physical and mental

readiness whether wanted or not don't come so often

sunlight slanting across pale blue sky toward ridge

white line of light reflected in motionless channel

5.25

blinding white circle of sun coming up beside ridge

blackness of crow standing on edge of redwood fence

condition of possibility which shows it can be both

also desire to see it again which one needs to move

one who turns what is seen across the channel ridge

blue sky water color tones on two-dimensional plane

blinding circle of sun in pale blue sky above ridge

horizontal white line of light reflected in channel

5.26

blinding edge of sun coming up above shadowed ridge

sound of crows calling back and forth in foreground

light this morning looking closely there's too much

thereby think of being present coincide with called

light and its absence in sunlit rose petal on right

behind paler pink white ones in shadowed foreground

shaft of light slanting across shadowed green ridge

white line of wave breaking on sand next to channel

5.27

white circle of sun in blue white sky next to ridge

blue jay standing on edge of shadowed redwood fence

space before further conditions light in place that

notes so as to interfere with text no other purpose

shape of right margin not essential line determined

not by visual shape but counting sound of syllables

blinding edge of sun in cloudless blue sky by ridge

white line of light reflected in motionless channel

5.28

gray whiteness of fog against still invisible ridge

crow landing on left edge of shadowed redwood fence

those called to serve further forced to return home

present call of passing confined to one point sight

one's mired down in inescapable earthbound concerns

other on ship bow sees sea and sky crossing Pacific

gray whiteness of fog still against invisible ridge

line of pelicans flapping from channel toward point

5.29

gray whiteness of fog against top of shadowed ridge

sound of unseen crow calling on branch across field

illustrated letter passed between sketch of present

something concealed in name not experienced thought

letter on desk whose last line read I wait to again

walk in the woods of our land with you dear comrade

gray whiteness of fog against still invisible ridge

line of pelicans flapping to the right toward point

5.30

gray whiteness of cloud slanting across green ridge

quail walking to the left across bricks below fence

petal there without a field rock that is a presence

see for the third time what about house in a letter

unseen heat lightning in window above sleeper's bed

followed by soft sound of thunder fading into night

blue opening of sky in clouds beside shadowed ridge

white line of wave breaking on sand next to channel

5.31

motionless gray clouds against shadowed green ridge

wingspan of crow flapping to the left toward branch

looking again flat glare sky in something I can see

subject called physical thought standing against it

huge wave washing through porthole reminding reader

Monet views of Notre Dame at different times of day

shadowed gray white clouds beside still black ridge

line of pelicans flapping to the right toward point

6.1

light gray whiteness of clouds against top of ridge

yellow of iris to the left of green glass back door

terms of light to be defined first two given events

way of moving certain thought references to subject

first moment startled into recognition then relaxes

second attentive way of holding the viewer in sight

gray white of clouds against invisible top of ridge

shadowed line of swell approaching mouth of channel

6.2

blinding circle of sun in pale blue sky above ridge

quail calling from corner of shadowed redwood fence

suffered further some of what continued observation

attention to look like the position of what it sees

one feeling sense of loss not being able to see son

so much has been lost it seems catches up sometimes

blinding white edge of sun beside shoulder of ridge

diagonal white line of wave breaking across channel

6.3

sun rising into cloudless pale blue sky above ridge

yellow of iris to the left of green glass back door

house in sunshine under sky subject yellow and blue

meaning of the word in dwelling speech falls silent

summer house in Corsica scorpions in shoes and beds

kept in jars to observe and feed and eventually die

white circle of sun in blue white sky next to ridge

sunlit white lines of waves breaking across channel

6.4

circle of sun by high thin white clouds above ridge

shadowed quail calling from corner of redwood fence

show how there set against it one and the same rock

letter the other day received next winter otherwise

last letter from this address cleaning out the desk

one's sense of shock growing at all that's happened

diagonal line of light slanting across toward ridge

V-shaped line of 8 pelicans flapping toward horizon

6.5

sun coming up in clouds beside shadowed green ridge

silhouette of crow landing on edge of redwood fence

size and form the picture's effect wider than other

physically experience of object as standing against

position of grass-colored deer in center foreground

having walked across dried grass field toward fence

sunlit white clouds against black shoulder of ridge

whiteness of wave breaking across windblown channel

6.6

blinding white of sun across from cloud above ridge

sound of crows calling back and forth in foreground

enter then in such a way reception the ray of light

confined to physical point of view concept of space

what makes being the thing thought of which is seen

relation of thought to position of physical remains

circle of sun above cloud next to shoulder of ridge

lines of waves breaking to the left next to channel

6.7

white circle of sun above white clouds beside ridge

motion of shadowed green leaves above redwood fence

time recalled that first meeting eye of tiny flower

simultaneity as if again and again position of same

object as thing in present condition of possibility

experience in same way here thought still beginning

sunlit white cloud in bright blue sky next to ridge

diagonal white line of wave breaking across channel

6.8

blinding white circle of sun coming up beside ridge

sound of crows calling back and forth in foreground

yellow house and the ground yellow too rough sketch

listen to what in the word thought following itself

thinking present of something less one then appears

responding in advance as the object present at hand

high thin white cloud across from shoulder of ridge

line of pelicans flapping to the right toward point

6.9

blinding edge of sun coming up above shadowed ridge

first unseen bird chirping from branch across field

clear that the same will appear another being means

revealing a feel for watching made the motion shown

different occurs in the clearing between here field

there in relation remains the present both together

whiteness of sun in cloudless blue sky beside ridge

V-shaped line of 12 pelicans gliding toward horizon

6.10

blinding whiteness of sun in fog above top of ridge

quail standing on redwood fence in right foreground

picture the actual measurement of form memory seems

presents itself as something the subject does there

depending on what you expect to see visualize scene

rather than reflect the leaves seem to absorb light

gray whiteness of fog against top of shadowed ridge

line of pelicans flapping to the right toward point

6.11

light gray whiteness of fog against invisible ridge

shadowed lavender across from green glass back door

finally in place of time light with respect to line

concept of page on the other hand concept of bodies

physical thought the appearance of having been here

between the naming of something and position behind

gray whiteness of fog against still invisible ridge

line of pelicans flapping to the right toward point

6.12

sun rising into clouds next to shadowed green ridge

motion of shadowed green bamboo leaves across fence

escape variety of subjects concentrate on first two

looking again at the same evidence in which appears

many hours of looking and working a moment position

elements come together state of simultaneous action

sun in whiteness of clouds beside shoulder of ridge

lines of pelicans gliding to the right toward point

6.13

sunlit and shadowed gray white clouds next to ridge

two crows landing on edge of shadowed redwood fence

later the house on the left green one in the shadow

ask what the building might be in its nature listen

how you can hear reader more sure how the line goes

slower marks the end with more emphasis how it hits

white of sun in cloud above black shoulder of ridge

lines and lines of pelicans flapping toward horizon

6.14

light gray whiteness of fog against invisible ridge

two house sparrows on shadowed fence next to feeder

how it will appear this way and that arranges world

other note records show painting not in house noted

throwing a series of events into the air the moment

letters arranged into words on two-dimensional page

gray whiteness of fog still against invisible ridge

lines of hundreds of pelicans flapping toward point

6.15

first edge of sun rising above shadowed green ridge

sound of crow calling on branch in right foreground

picture something in relation to whatever its shape

possible subject unfolds itself in forms of thought

first think of this position in this setting occurs

event between these and through come toward subject

blinding white sun in cloud above shoulder of ridge

lines of pelicans gliding from channel toward point

6.16

first white edge of sun rising above plane of ridge

blue jay standing on corner of fence next to feeder

system becomes condition extended from glance shows

sentence in the widest sense paper after rigid body

further the occurrence of noting rather than seeing

beginning of thinking which names itself being here

white circle of sun in bright blue sky beside ridge

line of pelicans flapping from point toward channel

6.17

blinding edge of sun rising above still black ridge

crows calling back and forth from branches in field

landscape at this time emphasis on foliage in field

shining body appears smoothness of informed subject

wind blowing the tops of sunlit trees across street

blue jay slanting to the right toward edge of fence

blinding whiteness of sun next to shoulder of ridge

lines of pelicans gliding from channel toward point

6.18

first white edge of sun rising above plane of ridge

two crows landing on edge of shadowed redwood fence

green tree at the end of the street painted picture

once more to remain in a place experience something

speaking of experience seen in each and every sense

imagine wave breaking against bulkhead next to bunk

pale blue whiteness of sky beside shoulder of ridge

line of pelicans flapping to the right toward point

6.19

light gray whiteness of fog against invisible ridge

3 crows standing on dried grass field in foreground

part outline of structure the object here and there

note letters by person relationship to what follows

blue-framed window on left wall of sunlit stairwell

light in the picture crossing the edge of its frame

gray whiteness of fog still against invisible ridge

line of 6 pelicans disappearing into fog on horizon

6.20

light gray whiteness of fog against invisible ridge

two sparrows landing on edge of fence beside feeder

frame of painting the space inside it different way

relation between these two for the most part facade

juxtaposition of two walls and a corner in sunlight

and shadow how the person's shadow stands on bricks

gray whiteness of fog against top of shadowed ridge

white line of wave breaking on sand next to channel

6.21

circle of sun rising in fog against invisible ridge

two birds chirping on branch somewhere across field

evident rotation in space see form before contained

after in which motion goes to show that such a body

sees the one imagined person standing here in front

painting in room angle of walls tilting up into sky

low gray whiteness of fog against shoulder of ridge

line of four pelicans gliding toward fog on horizon

6.22

gray whiteness of fog against still invisible ridge

crows calling back and forth from branches in field

trees reduce in scale the landscape come from hills

reading constructs the body of light extends beyond

taking the play back to the green world such things

action events known either first hand or by reading

gray whiteness of fog still against invisible ridge

wingspan of pelican flapping over windblown channel

6.23

gray whiteness of fog against still invisible ridge

shadowed lavender across from green glass back door

night to the left of remember beginning of a corner

thought of building something takes place before it

beginning of two moments in present today repeating

space with a blue green more than pale yellow green

gray whiteness of fog still against invisible ridge

two lines of pelicans gliding from point to channel

6.24

light gray whiteness of fog against invisible ridge

wind blowing bamboo branches next to shadowed fence

relate one to the other in itself therefore outside

see also the first image elements early passed away

same book on top of the others left corner of table

here also elsewhere table held together with a rope

gray whiteness of fog still against invisible ridge

lines of white waves breaking into mouth of channel

6.25

gray whiteness of fog still against invisible ridge

sound of crow calling from fence in left foreground

slow pull of sound from edge to edge of turn toward

feeling what is not counter to condition of subject

corner of a picture square matches the one opposite

arrives in a box behind the house birds in the dirt

gray whiteness of fog against top of shadowed ridge

diagonal white line of wave breaking across channel

6.26

light gray fog against still invisible top of ridge

black bee buzzing at lavender flowers in foreground

system in space taken as velocity relative to angle

rotation three degrees movement six or nine degrees

beginning in two moments of present today repeating

space with a blue green more than pale yellow green

gray whiteness of fog still against invisible ridge

lines of white waves breaking into mouth of channel

6.27

first light coming into fog against invisible ridge

sound of unknown bird calling from right foreground

vision in combination with one seen before his eyes

gained through part of dislocation a sense of flesh

see two calla lilies on the table kitchen reflected

in window black of night sounds in the outside dark

light gray fog against still invisible top of ridge

line of pelicans flapping from channel toward point

6.28

parallel white lines of clouds above shadowed ridge

bumble bee buzzing at lavender flower in foreground

midst of dog days beginning in May the yellow house

remaining in place turns to it each thing in nature

vertical crack in the sandstone-colored stucco wall

crow calling on edge of sunlit fence across from it

pale blue whiteness of sky beside shoulder of ridge

windblown white wave breaking into mouth of channel

6.29

gray whiteness of fog against top of shadowed ridge

three crows standing on edge of fence beside feeder

here between those and these mountains appear to me

there the figure as once before world flooded water

one sees to many things going all over the mountain

exactly not on the other hand an objective observer

light gray fog still against invisible top of ridge

line after line of pelicans flapping toward channel

6.30

blinding white circle of sun next to shadowed ridge

two quails pecking up seeds on bricks beside feeder

moment how narrow the plane between clumps of trees

thinking as what it already is coming to it belongs

pair of grape stakes in fence slanting to the right

against dry grass in field green plane of the ridge

line of sunlight against shadowed shoulder of ridge

four pelicans gliding across horizon toward channel

7.1

light gray whiteness of fog against invisible ridge

motion of shadowed green bamboo leaves across fence

first since it follows from these that form present

view of more or less bodies above number of degrees

chance of face on the page writing a body in motion

frogs barking in the dark asking moon where are you

sunlit gray white fog against top of shadowed ridge

line of 9 pelicans gliding toward windblown channel

7.2

light gray white fog against invisible top of ridge

quail pecking up seeds on bricks across from feeder

horizontal surface of the picture feeling landscape

location continuing through images of figure asleep

sense of feeling more lively in the morning charged

talking the other night continued through yesterday

gray whiteness of fog against top of shadowed ridge

windblown white wave breaking into mouth of channel

7.3

gray whiteness of fog against top of shadowed ridge

blue jay slanting toward edge of bricks below fence

yellow place used until moved in drawing of subject

reflect in the sense of stay on earth under the sky

out of the ground is also there everything standing

stands in the event however many times has happened

gray white line of fog against still shadowed ridge

line of pelicans flapping to the right toward point

7.4

white circle of sun in cloud next to shadowed ridge

bee on lavender flower beside green glass back door

condition of there the present itself and the other

person sees asks you where this was called movement

picture views this way then that opposite direction

lines of bricks in path next to hedge in the middle

sunlit clouds in pale blue sky by shoulder of ridge

white line of wave breaking on sand next to channel

7.5

blinding white circle of sun coming up beside ridge

bees landing on lavender flowers in left foreground

inside space the foreground flows from side to side

subject a form of self thinking that sees in a note

focusing on a moment in which arrangement is a part

sunlit pair of vertical windows in still black wall

cloudless pale blue sky beside black slope of ridge

white line of wave breaking on sand next to channel

7.6

blinding white circle of sun above tree-lined ridge

leaves on bamboo branch moving in wind across fence

system follows from fact depends on right hand side

motion of body relatively sense plays the same part

arrangement of lines viewed by eye moving down page

minimal movement from 3 lines to 2 becomes enormous

lines of sunlight in cloudless blue sky above ridge

lines and lines of pelicans flapping toward channel

7.7

blinding circle of sun in pale blue sky above ridge

two sparrows landing on feeder beside redwood fence

compare the name of other look with eye at pictures

know the meaning of why process of disjointed sides

now full moon comes up out there in black night sky

picture of it rises from behind eucalyptus branches

white circle of sun next to black shoulder of ridge

wingspan of pelican flapping overhead above channel

7.8

blinding circle of sun in pale blue sky above ridge

unseen bee buzzing at lavender flower in foreground

making the house in water color at the edge of town

both of these also means belonging with one another

two sparrows standing on left edge of redwood fence

one flaps toward bamboo branch the other follows it

shaft of sunlight slanting toward shoulder of ridge

line of eleven pelicans gliding across toward point

7.9

white circle of sun rising into clouds beside ridge

bees feeding on lavender flowers in left foreground

whether or not I decide to take in stride a subject

before the years which pass from shadows into light

when syntax becomes different in relation to things

something being talked about also becomes different

sunlit white clouds in blue white sky next to ridge

whiteness of wave breaking across windblown channel

7.10

blinding white circle of sun next to shadowed ridge

sound of crow calling on branch in right foreground

by contrast the zigzag path where man sits sideways

relation of object to concept of subject understood

two views of sunlit also shadowed sandstone-colored

corner of wall shadow of someone standing on bricks

sun in gray whiteness of fog against shadowed ridge

lines of white waves breaking into mouth of channel

7.11

white circle of sun rising beside cloud above ridge

bee landing on lavender flowers by green glass door

multiplied by a factor of moving in direction of it

sense of the body second to last two angles follows

shadowed left edge of sandstone-colored stucco wall

first picture corner next to side facing the viewer

circle of sun in fog against invisible top of ridge

line of pelicans flapping to the right toward point

7.12

blinding white of sun in pale blue sky beside ridge

bee feeding on lavender flowers by green glass door

several flowers one resembles at first glance paint

may not seem answers perhaps different side effects

not to think of the ground which is determined less

between an event appears in the room of the subject

light gray white fog against invisible top of ridge

line after line of pelicans flapping toward channel

7.13

blinding edge of sun beside shadowed slope of ridge

crows calling back and forth from shadowed branches

near the house torn down the other sent in a letter

one belonging together spread out in rock and water

something about how letters put together into words

placed in lines enter mind of reader who reads them

white line of cloud in blue white sky next to ridge

line after line of pelicans flapping toward horizon

7.14

light gray whiteness of fog against invisible ridge

quail pecking up seeds from bricks by redwood fence

place on the earth's surface thinking point of view

day as one day month after month both of themselves

a matter of standing outside sense of losing ground

sound of something here appears being what is given

gray whiteness of fog against top of shadowed ridge

lines and lines of pelicans flapping toward horizon

7.15

light gray whiteness of fog against invisible ridge

silhouette of sparrow perched on fence above feeder

movement to the right space open dark against light

idea of subject includes itself as long as we think

first measure according to which follows everything

ground that becomes even more at the same time less

gray whiteness of fog against top of shadowed ridge

line of pelicans gliding to the left toward channel

7.16

gray whiteness of fog against still invisible ridge

bee landing on lavender flowers by green glass door

measured rest equal to motion with respect to space

follows from position of place distances from there

motionless shapes of flowers next to telephone pole

background a dream caught in the act of fading away

light gray white fog against invisible top of ridge

wingspan of pelican gliding overhead toward horizon

7.17

gray whiteness of fog still against invisible ridge

quail pecking up seeds on bricks across from feeder

painting of flowers seem to be an object on a table

question of something experienced as if to say look

edge of viewer's left shoulder shadows intersecting

motion of sunlit lavender on sandstone-colored wall

gray whiteness of fog against top of shadowed ridge

line of pelicans flapping to the right toward point

7.18

gray whiteness of fog against still invisible ridge

bee hovering above lavender beside green glass door

recorded in a book between see repetition and paper

say we think of the other three thought one of four

what happens when one sees two views of green hedge

again and again seems to be senses changing in time

gray whiteness of fog against top of shadowed ridge

line of pelicans gliding to the left toward channel

7.19

gray whiteness of fog against top of shadowed ridge

bees landing on lavender flowers by green back door

here what is more to see things still to experience

when they pass from shadow into light italics added

when bird flies in open glass back door hits window

above table flies out again fog lifts against ridge

light gray fog against still invisible top of ridge

line of pelicans gliding to the left across horizon

7.20

gray whiteness of fog against top of shadowed ridge

quail walking around on bricks beside redwood fence

figures in foreground happen in sense flow of space

see this time the present subject as already passed

experience everything in relation to something else

imagining shadow of person on wall in fog not there

gray whiteness of fog against top of shadowed ridge

line of five pelicans gliding across toward horizon

7.21

white edge of sun in fog against top of green ridge

red finches perched on feeder next to redwood fence

make shape of bodies relative to direction in space

therefore the form further right together identical

form which is the opposite of what is to be thought

first the talk of event places return to the ground

light gray fog against still invisible top of ridge

line of pelicans flapping to the right toward point

7.22

gray whiteness of fog against top of shadowed ridge

three crows standing on edge of fence beside feeder

in this way appears an arrangement of every element

experienced making that which keeps turning my head

get everything in the mind into eye patterns become

trees reflected in water symmetrical to trees above

gray white fog against still invisible top of ridge

lines and lines of pelicans flapping toward horizon

7.23

fog still against invisible top of tree-lined ridge

house sparrow standing on fence in right foreground

water in drawn frame found letter as part of window

thought of the sky path of sun moon wandering stars

facts including how one chooses path down the cliff

rope to counteract gravity face of approaching wave

motionless light gray fog against shoulder of ridge

V-shaped line of 9 pelicans flapping toward channel

7.24

blinding whiteness sun in cloudless sky above ridge

red finch pecking up seeds from bricks below feeder

feet in a way which choose possible objects include

next time early light see history of meaning visual

exploration of space moving from this point to that

each letter an event in place between eye and thing

white line of fog below bright blue sky above ridge

diagonal white line of wave breaking across channel

7.25

light gray white fog against invisible top of ridge

two crows pecking up seeds from bricks below feeder

gesture here stands for picture ebb and flow events

ground the beginning of what appears in relation to

form which is the opposite of what is to be thought

first the talk of event places return to the ground

gray white fog against still invisible top of ridge

whiteness of wave breaking across windblown channel

7.26

light gray whiteness of fog against invisible ridge

two finches perched on feeder next to redwood fence

motion of space in reference to its lateral surface

point between front and back arranged to be earlier

view of horizontal white wave breaking on far shore

sunlit lower edge of fog parallel relative to ridge

flat gray plane of fog against still shadowed ridge

line of pelicans flapping from channel toward point

7.27

light gray whiteness of fog against invisible ridge

house sparrow perched on edge of fence above feeder

under the flower two angles first at top of picture

expose the subject sound the opposite of all things

visual pattern of letters one sees but doesn't hear

two crows in relation to crows below shadowed fence

white circle of sun in fog beside shoulder of ridge

diagonal white line of wave breaking across channel

7.28

gray whiteness of fog still against invisible ridge

house sparrow lifting from fence to feeder below it

place transferred to selected color before painting

changes the light of day drifting clouds blue depth

starting to feel the day is beginning to get warmer

same way how to pronounce the word father as father

diaçonal edge of pale blue sky in fog against ridge

line of pelicans flapping from point toward channel

7.29

light gray whiteness of fog against invisible ridge

sound of crow calling on branch in right foreground

system in which the tree appears other than subject

for use of light in form of see some as told to say

those trees over there in which light green grasses

oval around which cars are parked whoever left them

gray whiteness of fog against top of shadowed ridge

line of pelicans flapping to the right toward point

7.30

light gray white fog against invisible top of ridge

quail walking across bricks by feeder next to fence

moment the sun rises belonging to something as well

perception of a certain way of being found in sound

one letter after the other lines an apparent stream

sometimes in a normal voice reading anyway you want

gray whiteness of fog against top of shadowed ridge

small south swell wave breaking in mouth of channel

7.31

gray whiteness of fog against top of shadowed ridge

house sparrow perched on edge of fence above feeder

last two more than lateral surface referred to here

later than traces of light an event causes an event

green at the same time each day the surface changes

pictures earth's position in relation to sun or fog

light gray whiteness fog still against top of ridge

lines and lines of pelicans flapping toward horizon

8.1

white circle of sun above line of fog against ridge

bees landing on lavender flowers in left foreground

farthest right white flower second from left formed

holds up to what was made becomes an index of given

sound of distant voices whose emotion can't be felt

music in background something like feeling in chest

blinding white sun above fog against shadowed ridge

sunlit white lines of waves breaking across channel

8.2

whiteness of sun in fog above still invisible ridge

bees landing on lavender flowers in left foreground

water made before summer September considered first

sky thinking of the other three thought one of four

walking across far side of the room between windows

view of dried grasses on the ridge middle of summer

faint white of sun in fog against shoulder of ridge

sound of white wave breaking on sand beside channel

8.3

white edge of sun next to tree-lined green of ridge

two deer walking in line across field in foreground

surrounding in a double sense the mountain as shown

out of time here after turned to more than it found

witness almost full moon comes up after days of fog

man who passed away would have but now won't see it

blinding whiteness of sun next to shoulder of ridge

small white waves breaking across windblown channel

8.4

light coming into fog against still invisible ridge

motion of shadowed green bamboo leaves across fence

moment in space measure something a gesture repeats

sound conditions the object sounds like saying that

how view out window shows what one is talking about

space made of lines including time a note to itself

gray whiteness of fog still against invisible ridge

wingspan of pelican gliding across mouth of channel

8.5

gray whiteness of clouds against top of green ridge

six baby quails running across bricks beside feeder

measures the action of system moves in direction of

point between effect conveyed the velocity of light

sensation of saying color becomes place in painting

motion of shadowed green of leaves on redwood fence

gray white cloud against shadowed shoulder of ridge

line after line of pelicans flapping toward horizon

8.6

light coming into fog against still invisible ridge

two quails pecking up seeds on bricks below fence

orange flower at farthest left round leaf at bottom

recall the answer point to that place image in time

overhead view of pattern of shadowed tips of leaves

leading into another green thought in a green shade

gray whiteness of fog still against invisible ridge

line of pelicans flapping to the right toward point

8.7

licht gray whiteness of fog against invisible ridge

house sparrow standing on rose branch in foreground

draw image after paint promise to send small sketch

clouds the way head appears speak of thinking three

someone else in other clothes talks to other people

one who dreams about something that hasn't happened

gray whiteness of fog still against invisible ridge

line of pelicans flapping to the right toward point

8.8

light gray whiteness of fog against invisible ridge

two house sparrows standing on feeder in foreground

shape perceived between pair one figure and another

more later practice notes the following translation

way home after social distance visit below overlook

person finding the body fallen off bike on hawthorn

gray whiteness of fog still against invisible ridge

3 cormorants flapping across channel toward horizon

8.9

first light coming into fog against invisible ridge

motionless black bamboo branch across redwood fence

spaces surface around the end let the feeling occur

sounds the present subject shows itself and appears

how mind's echoing through process becomes interior

interaction of voices an extension of linear sounds

gray whiteness of fog against still invisible ridge

lines of waves breaking to the right across channel

8.10

light coming into pale blue sky above granite peaks

sound of water falling on rocks in right foreground

negative of twice since equal to measure it follows

relative to system in which effect later than cause

how one notices switching something from two to one

was it or were they present in that room of persons

blue whiteness of sky beside sunlit triangular peak

moon above shadowed granite ridge to the left of it

8.11

pink red orange of sunlight on triangular gray peak

white half moon in cloudless pale blue sky overhead

second painting see at visual center of arrangement

measure of the figure in a moment some such emotion

something about visual less as color than stillness

relative to the fact of things happening over there

plane of granite ridge reflected in motionless lake

white patch of snow on left side of triangular peak

8.12

light coming into sky above triangular granite peak

reflection of rocks across motionless shadowed lake

after view including the differences between colors

along with thought one called thinking of the other

person in another room picking up the phone to call

expecting no one is there to answer leaving message

cloudless blue white sky by triangular granite peak

shadowed white snow on the ridge to the right of it

8.13

horizontal line of white cloud above shadowed ridge

sunlit slope of triangular gray peak across from it

other as if the side of someone such and such given

see also the present what is there beginning second

grounded in relation to whether these matters today

background present in the way this establishes fact

blinding white edge of sun above blackness of peaks

motionless lake's surface below peak across from it

8.14

first light coming into sky above blackness of peak

upturned curve of waning moon to the left of planet

space on the tip of the tongue forearm straight out

call which of all things shown itself in such a way

left hand falling forward one when talking about it

as if ideas were something that had happened to him

motionless black lake against vertical granite wall

sound of one bird chirping somewhere across from it

8.15

first light coming into sky above still black peaks

upturned curve of waning moon to the left of planet

system of possibility considered in previous motion

may be changed so that comes to be earlier than say

think of what occurred on the surface of the ground

figure returned emptied of all but water in a glass

vertical granite peaks reflected in motionless lake

diagonal lines of clouds above peaks across from it

8.16

gray white rain cloud above shadowed green of ridge

motionless bamboo leaves moving above redwood fence

center point the other square triangles in painting

ground seems hard to deny last points to difference

right square corner of picture matches its opposite

thinking it might arrives in a box behind the house

gray lines of rain falling toward shoulder of ridge

diagonal white line of wave breaking across channel

8.17

sunlit edge of gray rain cloud above shadowed ridge

two sparrows landing on redwood fence beside feeder

observe the presence in shapes which suggest change

resemblance between double description of two parts

past the horizon of the present there slipping away

object as a consequence of apparent light something

gray plane of cloud moving toward shoulder of ridge

white line of wave breaking across mouth of channel

8.18

white circle of sun rising into clouds beside ridge

sound of crow calling on branch in right foreground

series between figures echoes of arms and shoulders

appearance of coming here lets it become what it is

words taking on momentum interior to what is spoken

towhee lifting from branch whose motion echoes this

blinding white circle of sun in cloud above channel

line of pelicans flapping to the right toward point

8.19

reddish pink of sun rising into smoke next to ridge

three birds perched on redwood fence next to feeder

measuring the position of points follows from first

may be chosen in ways that become the idea of after

asleep in the margin tilting toward time remembered

window in whose light one rests slips into swimming

whiteness of sun in smoke next to shoulder of ridge

diagonal white line of wave breaking across channel

8.20

light coming into fog beside shadowed tops of trees

wingspan of pelican flapping toward invisible ridge

flowers made to form such element fit into the plan

points between the period and form appear in action

gray white fog in sky more than half aspect of view

doesn't include the unseen ridge viewer who sees it

diagonal gray line of fog against shoulder of ridge

line of pelicans flapping to the right toward point

8.21

gray whiteness of fog against still invisible ridge

motion of bamboo leaves in wind above redwood fence

color the first note after the difference in detail

thinking one of four something more than sky as sky

frame later to mention letter give an idea of color

speaking of thought in the way the word still known

sunlit gray white fog still against invisible ridge

lines and lines of birds flapping across from point

8.22

gray whiteness of fog against still invisible ridge

green motion of bamboo leaves next to redwood fence

meaning capable of anything hesitant chooses itself

correspondence from the world of movement describes

color of lake's water and sky so close to same blue

two horizontal lines of far shore in the foreground

light gray whiteness of fog against invisible ridge

lines of pelicans gliding to the right toward point

8.23

light gray whiteness of fog against invisible ridge

two towhees pecking up seeds on bricks below feeder

slightly different more once seen measure of figure

one hand beginning the last light on the other only

appearance of place in which moment becomes smaller

sense also physical as object disappears to nothing

gray whiteness of fog against still invisible ridge

white line of wave breaking on sand next to channel

8.24

gray whiteness of fog against still invisible ridge

two sparrows standing on redwood fence above feeder

clock at rest when observed follows from the second

one signal to be sent the second event at the point

person's image recalling image referred to as event

washed hair the cause rather than effect of emotion

light gray whiteness of fog against invisible ridge

V-shaped line of cormorants flapping toward horizon

8.25

gray whiteness of fog against top of shadowed ridge

blue jay landing on edge of redwood fence by feeder

other evident painting suggests placed five objects

count the later present one body outside the figure

kind of leaning back against an unseen granite rock

blood on right leg crossed over left taking a break

gray whiteness of fog still against invisible ridge

lines of gulls flapping to the right toward horizon

8.26

gray whiteness of fog still against invisible ridge

two sparrows standing on redwood fence above feeder

changed earlier reference two colors made in spring

sun and moon to star to season night to day to rest

sun shining through smoke and fog so much alike one

has smell the other doesn't birds flapping by in it

gray whiteness of fog against still invisible ridge

sound of waves breaking on sand across from channel

8.27

first light coming into fog against invisible ridge

motionless black bamboo leaves above shadowed fence

directions and possibilities drawn by looking at it

acted as part at this time see relation to describe

boulder below peaks against streaks of white clouds

hard to imagine impossible to capture in photograph

light coming into fog against still invisible ridge

sound of waves breaking on sand across from channel

8.28

first light coming into fog against invisible ridge

motionless black bamboo branch above shadowed fence

movement in space reaching further arm balance body

later physical position in light of nearly possible

stance of being toward as well as reverse then what

grounded on something itself counter to that can be

gray whiteness of fog still against invisible ridge

sound of swell line breaking on sand beside channel

8.29

light gray whiteness of fog against invisible ridge

sound of crow calling on branch in right foreground

follows and shows the clock goes slower relative to

after velocity of light impossible to set in motion

everything here moves behind a semblance of objects

say the echo belongs to the event one becomes other

gray whiteness of fog against top of shadowed ridge

white line of wave breaking on sand next to channel

8.30

orange circle of sun in fog against invisible ridge

two sparrows standing on edge of fence above feeder

flat picture plane center indicate by diagonal line

evidence of sides condition unobserved before again

objects lost in the whirl of circling close to burn

event come to smolder danger still not come to ruin

circle of sun in fog against invisible top of ridge

line of 9 pelicans gliding in from point to channel

8.31

first light coming into fog against invisible ridge

motionless black bamboo leaves across redwood fence

first color the same function image of yellow house

holding the darkening sky looking where it would be

everything that is nothing less than its occurrence

first itself brings at the same time keeps in sight

gray whiteness of fog against still invisible ridge

line of 7 pelicans gliding to the left toward point

9.1

light coming into fog against top of shadowed ridge

red-shouldered hawk calling on branch in foreground

collection of things which emerge from a background

steps that led to letters memory of relation to see

state of nature finding likewise all previous views

beyond approach to question of physical possibility

gray white fog against still invisible top of ridge

sound of waves breaking on sand across from channel

9.2

gray whiteness of fog against still invisible ridge

line of 7 sparrows on shadowed fence next to feeder

right leg moving forward the difference between two

recall the appearance of coming that one might mean

line going on and on object going on until it stops

how one notices change in something from two to one

gray whiteness of fog against top of shadowed ridge

V-shaped line of 9 pelicans flapping toward channel

9.3

first light coming into fog against invisible ridge

wind beginning to move bamboo branches beside fence

sequence of two systems which take the place of one

set in a distant place velocity of light understood

gathered a presence in the first place here and now

beginning to count the object still could be called

gray whiteness of fog still against invisible ridge

diagonal white line of wave breaking across channel

9.4

light gray whiteness of fog against invisible ridge

sound of quail calling Chi-ca-go in left foreground

shadow on light line comes to edge of white picture

see what they are about whatever these figures seem

where the present takes over at the same time still

relation of things included alongside other objects

sunlit white edge fog against still invisible ridge

white line of wave breaking across mouth of channel

9.5

red orange circle of sun above still shadowed ridge

red-shouldered hawk calling on branch in foreground

some idea of color as red and green yellow and blue

means to look after something attached to something

question of relation to form also what does it mean

subject begin such and such equal to being under it

blinding circle of sun in pale blue sky above ridge

terns circling and diving across motionless channel

9.6

blinding edge of sun rising above still black ridge

first bird landing on feeder next to shadowed fence

forms presenting themselves to be touched beyond us

see almost however name at the end of second letter

something itself more than given in a different way

relation to answer naming possible at the same time

white circle of sun next to black shoulder of ridge

diagonal white line of wave breaking across channel

9.7

blinding white circle of sun next to shadowed ridge

waning white moon in bright blue sky by rose branch

action which may on the face of it be more distinct

nature a word for what is named coming forth slowly

moment of time fallen into abyss no answer in sight

position in itself even when we want to be not said

white circle of sun rising beside shoulder of ridge

terns circling and diving toward motionless channel

9.8

gray whiteness of fog smoke against invisible ridge

two towhees pecking up seeds on bricks below feeder

statement about variant form same dimensional space

periodic on the other hand two points and two lines

sense of occurrence physical thought back to origin

line being nothing other than everything once again

yellow red orange sun in smoke by shoulder of ridge

line of 7 pelicans flapping across channel to point

9.9

reddish orange of fog smoke against invisible ridge

motionless black bamboo branch across redwood fence

mark diagonal crosses from top left to bottom right

looks of parts from points a change of mood sets in

connection between felt tone and that which thought

reaches a peak sees itself touch something in sound

orange of smoke against invisible shoulder of ridge

sound of terns circling to the right across channel

9.10

light coming into fog smoke against invisible ridge

3 sparrows standing on edge of fence next to feeder

dependence on present tone and light touch of color

how things at any time themselves in their presence

made at home objects turn even the earth into other

figure as action beyond or beside called such again

gray whiteness of fog against still invisible ridge

line of 6 pelicans flapping across channel to point

9.11

gray whiteness of fog smoke against invisible ridge

motionless green bamboo leaves above shadowed fence

conscious of thoughts in world therefore themselves

see also three views concerned with material object

sky here too apocalyptic orange seemed to stay dark

all day yesterday an early winter evening 5 o'clock

reddish pink sun in smoke against shoulder of ridge

line of pelicans disappearing in fog across channel

9.12

light gray whiteness of fog against invisible ridge

3 sparrows pecking up seeds from bricks below fence

look on face action that goes with resisting nature

translation far from form of experience might bring

somehow in the future which is now present now past

dog who can barely get up from his bed next to wall

gray whiteness of fog still against invisible ridge

sound of waves breaking on sand across from channel

9.13

gray whiteness of smoke fog against invisible ridge

3 sparrows pecking up seeds from feeder below fence

continuum as unit of measure given a pair of events

parallel to system of reference compared with point

hears when the room gets still again measured water

analogous in that logic determined by person in bed

pale gray white fog smoke against shoulder of ridge

line of pelicans flapping from channel toward point

9.14

gray whiteness of fog smoke against invisible ridge

silhouette of sparrow on edge of fence above feeder

opposite lines of shadow cast by table leg below it

aspect from vantage point toward following thoughts

what one wants to take home finds in precise moment

looking down to the left a newspaper in the doorway

pale gray fog smoke still against shoulder of ridge

terns circling to the left above motionless channel

9.15

light coming into sky smoke above still black ridge

upturned curve of waning moon to the left of planet

various additions made view sight on street of road

how is this done in this way in the narrowing sense

in other words all but impermeable to sunlight rain

fog or smoke that keeps things so gray this morning

whiteness of sun in smoke next to shoulder of ridge

wingspan of pelican gliding over motionless channel

9.16

light gray whiteness of fog against invisible ridge

two sparrows landing on shadowed fence above feeder

self which is not some subject runs ahead of itself

word less used before the first use here is aimless

seeing appearance of Perseid meteors after sun sets

otherwise things coming to pass in words being said

gray whiteness of fog against still invisible ridge

lines and lines of cormorants flapping toward point

9.17

light gray whiteness of fog against invisible ridge

4 sparrows standing on shadowed fence beside feeder

other action tries to make space which is contained

in order to be close to approach of what is closest

return to relation which includes isolation of both

thinking first at the same time what can be touched

gray whiteness of fog still against invisible ridge

white line of wave breaking across mouth of channel

9.18

yellow red orange of clouds above still black ridge

red-shouldered hawk calling on branch in foreground

number of dimensions in the following only when two

clock in motion gives time corresponding to instant

concept of being as objects present position ground

beginning thought return to everything that follows

gray whiteness of fog against top of shadowed ridge

diagonal white line of wave breaking across channel

9.19

yellow orange edge of sun next to still black ridge

sparrow flapping from rose branch to shadowed fence

parallel paintings of figures surface flat as a map

parts of the face intersect in space look less like

light on second from left walnut tree trunk drawing

viewer who wants to see bark more closely toward it

blinding circle of sun in pale blue sky above ridge

line of pelicans flapping to the right toward point

9.20

blinding yellow circle of sun coming up above ridge

sparrow landing on edge of fence across from feeder

streamline view descriptive details picture at left

build four things on our way to the second question

locate thought in perception of shadow of table leg

outside the mind that lies along bricks below fence

circular white sun in fog against shoulder of ridge

sound of waves breaking on sand across from channel

9.21`

light gray whiteness of fog against invisible ridge

motion of shadowed green bamboo leaves across fence

relation to things in order form such as perception

second of several for example sixteen also the same

when clarity doesn't require stops to differentiate

walking also what one sees and thinks along the way

gray whiteness of fog against top of shadowed ridge

line of pelicans flapping from point toward channel

9.22

white circle of sun in bright blue sky beside ridge

sparrow on fence next to bamboo leaves above feeder

say direction goes away turning space in foreground

toward which thinking now of time as letting appear

too dark in the house to take the picture one wants

color of words on paper outside under orange of sky

blinding white of sun in light blue sky above ridge

white line of wave breaking across mouth of channel

9.23

white circle of sun in trees against shadowed ridge

three house sparrows perched on feeder beside fence

points together on the other hand variant condition

always moving changes of direction stationary point

parallel look of matches stacked on a granite table

arrangement that might fly apart scatter after time

blinding white sun coming up over shoulder of ridge

line of pelicans flapping to the right toward point

9.24

light gray whiteness of fog against invisible ridge

4 sparrows lined up on edge of fence next to feeder

geometric surface adding a certain form as if drawn

sheets intersecting in space suggest the transposed

shift of perspective from direction moving to place

shadows in motion of bamboo leaves on redwood fence

sun in cloudless blue sky next to fog against ridge

line of pelicans flapping from point across channel

9.25

planet rising into predawn sky above black of ridge

motionless black bamboo leaves above shadowed fence

picture legible type at right yellow house on paper

long answer to question sense of constructing thing

shadow of plastic tape on window across words shows

how to ground thought in perception of what's there

yellow orange edge of sky next to shoulder of ridge

shadowed white line of wave breaking across channel

9.26

planet in faint gray white sky above plane of ridge

first sparrow perched on feeder below edge of fence

ground person in such perceptions something present

sound of abstract painting positions now come about

following the brightness shines on its own one sees

account of the ground light somehow also concealing

white circle of sun next to black shoulder of ridge

swell line moving toward windblown mouth of channel

9.27

yellow pink orange edge of sky above plane of ridge

two sparrows landing on shadowed fence above feeder

painting over space a little like way of repetition

reference to being in the open attempt to follow it

writing possible objects to construct whole present

less about content of fragments after thinking here

blinding white line of sun reflected across channel

wingspan of gull flapping to the right toward point

9.28

orange of sun in branches against still black ridge

two shadowed sparrows on edge of fence above feeder

points connected by light events presented in space

moving therefore actual motion formed of particular

how one sees what one notices in what one perceives

motion of shadowed green bamboo leaves across fence

white circle of sun next to black shoulder of ridge

sound of waves breaking on sand across from channel

9.29

light gray whiteness of fog against invisible ridge

7 sparrows lined up on edge of fence next to feeder

space reduced to its form echoes effect of painting

again in light shows the figure proposed as subject

sound of tone and meaning of word following horizon

distinction between what is said and mood of object

gray whiteness of fog against still invisible ridge

lines of gulls flapping to the right toward horizon

9.30

gray whiteness of fog against top of shadowed ridge

crow flapping from across field in right foreground

letters you see in present house some idea of color

building in the sense of things example reflections

fall leaves fallen on sidewalk a deep reddish brown

camera can't capture the color the eye sees it sees

sunlit white edges of fog against shoulder of ridge

line after line of pelicans flapping toward channel

10.1

gray whiteness of fog smoke against invisible ridge

sparrow slanting from feeder to field in foreground

something present at a given moment midst of things

moment that today remains concealed see view period

fragment at times instead of having words preserved

given a way of moving toward shimmer that brightens

reddish circle of sun in smoke by shoulder of ridge

line of pelicans flapping from point toward channel

10.2

yellow red orange sun rising into smoke above ridge

sparrow pecking up seeds from bricks next to feeder

ground level light how sun in picture to talk about

thinking ahead the word makes first what is thought

sound of word traced back to acoustic and emotional

object of meaning a matter of part of body thinking

blinding white sun in smoke above shoulder of ridge

line of pelicans flapping from point toward channel

10.3

gray whiteness of fog against still invisible ridge

3 sparrows standing on edge of fence next to feeder

event present by means of light upper half of point

compare circle become in real time imaginary motion

entering into accomplishment of event comes to pass

disappearing and coming back perhaps from elsewhere

white circle of sun above line of fog against ridge

line of white wave breaking across mouth of channel

10.4

light coming into fog against still invisible ridge

sparrow pecking up seeds from bricks next to feeder

without perspective two bottles almost totally flat

figure at first present position front away from it

whether to think after what thought from a distance

relation to difference between the object and place

gray whiteness of fog still against invisible ridge

line of 6 pelicans disappearing into fog on horizon

10.5

light gray whiteness of fog against invisible ridge

motion of shadowed green bamboo leaves across fence

drawing on paper water part place transfer to place

as bridge crosses the stream one side against other

cloud moves across tops of trees makes wind visible

moment of sparrow slanting from fence toward bricks

gray whiteness of fog still against invisible ridge

line of 4 pelicans flapping into fog across channel

10.6

light gray whiteness of fog against invisible ridge

circular pink white rose on edge of fence by feeder

heat of the sun feeling all this light object touch

appeared in period given by letter content and form

sun comes up makes three words one time progression

motion follows one after another as still as can be

gray whiteness of fog against still invisible ridge

line of pelicans disappearing in fog across channel

10.7

gray whiteness of fog against top of shadowed ridge

blue jay pecking up seeds from feeder next to fence

morning more than instance what happens among trees

in this way a consequence opening up whether or not

cloud moves across tops of trees makes wind visible

moment of sparrow slanting from fence toward bricks

sunlit edges of gray white fog against top of ridge

two pelicans flapping across horizon toward channel

10.8

light comes into fog against invisible top of ridge

sound of golden-crowned sparrows calling oh dear me

light sent from lower half points from which can be

kind of motion given three points constant distance

elsewhere further over there shadowed bamboo leaves

move on table crows calling back and forth far away

gray whiteness of fog against top of shadowed ridge

line of pelicans flapping to the right toward point

10.9

light gray whiteness of fog against invisible ridge

two sparrows perched on feeder beside edge of fence

picture other objects by placement forward in space

front and back graphic expression of image on paper

sun and moon and sun seen in relation to each other

seems to be moving up then down from frame to frame

blinding whiteness of sun next to cloud above ridge

pelicans flapping to the left from point to channel

10.10

gray whiteness of clouds above shadowed green ridge

two sparrows on edge of redwood fence beside feeder

first letter sent to selected date related painting

example of border brings to the landscape behind it

living hand holding pen moves across the white page

curve of orchid branch next to leaves on windowsill

gray whiteness of fog above black shoulder of ridge

line of pelicans flapping from point toward channel

10.11

light coming into blue whiteness of sky above ridge

waning white moon across from branches beside fence

object brings to different manner of being in world

included notes unable to attach meaning to sentence

two words saying the same thing name which is thing

listen to saying even more think different thinking

blinding whiteness of sun next to shoulder of ridge

line after line of pelicans flapping toward horizon

10.12

cloudless blue white sky above still shadowed ridge

two towhees pecking up seeds on bricks below feeder

holding left side glimpse green marks between trees

open in the first place prior to all we need to see

entering into an appearance also to be or not to be

concealed in the sense of submerge optical illusion

red orange of sun coming up above shoulder of ridge

V-shaped line of 12 pelicans gliding toward channel

10.13

white circle of sun rising behind branches of trees

sound of golden-crowned sparrows calling oh dear me

surface negative as well as present possible motion

line touched by curve of note multiplied as follows

thinking in view of the fact that a house or a tree

movement from one to the other sometimes approaches

blinding whiteness of sun next to shoulder of ridge

white line of wave breaking on sand next to channel

10.14

light coming into blue whiteness of sky above ridge

silhouette of sparrow perched on fence above feeder

viewer reaching into the distance position in space

adapt to painting one view at a time since standing

what is thought called more than others think shows

appear in the name bringing to appearance to itself

blinding whiteness of sun next to shoulder of ridge

lines of pelican flapping toward motionless channel

10.15

pinkish yellow edge of sky beside still black ridge

motion of shadowed green bamboo leaves beside fence

one of the last made referred to in letter describe

brings into each gathers as landscape around stream

sense of toward which called appears here and there

how in a different way when there for the most part

blinding whiteness of sun next to shoulder of ridge

line of pelicans flapping toward motionless channel

10.16

light coming into gray blue white sky next to ridge

shadowed green of bamboo leaves moving beside fence

others in relation to here once more at each moment

original words both of which color also means paint

previous view after thinking of spoken and unspoken

present something names a figure connection between

blinding white circle of sun coming up beside ridge

line of pelicans gliding to the left across channel

10.17

pale blue gray white sky above still shadowed ridge

sound of golden-crowned sparrows calling oh dear me

line of trees the way a second light between levels

experience of something made it speak some way here

follows the story only what must be said hands down

unfolds together with that which appears and shines

blinding red orange of sun beside shoulder of ridge

line of pelicans flapping to the right toward point

10.18

light coming into gray blue white sky next to ridge

faint white planet to the left of shadowed branches

velocity less than light in the direction of motion

moment defined by notes as elsewhere equal to force

shadows of bamboo leaves moving over lines on paper

seeing again and again everything happening at once

blinding white circle of sun coming up beside ridge

line after line of pelicans flapping toward channel

10.19

gray whiteness of fog against still invisible ridge

two sparrows landing on edge of fence beside feeder

pictorial space far from reflected approach to note

simultaneity of face and body again and again image

presence being present the way the eye lights on it

looking again at how everything happens all at once

gray whiteness of fog still against invisible ridge

line of pelicans disappearing in fog across channel

10.20

gray whiteness of sky still against invisible ridge

7 sparrows standing on edge of fence next to feeder

painting found in vantage point places made between

resting in stream's bed waters run from sky's flood

event the notion of becoming object possible ground

subject later also the form position between points

light gray whiteness of fog against invisible ridge

three pelicans disappearing into fog across channel

10.21

first light coming into sky above still black ridge

brightness of planet to the left of shadowed branch

word to make way for it here once more toward world

translation of sentence parallel to first assertion

ordinary presence in the everyday thereby encounter

what here and how remain in the same light possible

pink red yellow edge of sky above shoulder of ridge

white line of wave breaking on sand next to channel

10.22

light coming into fog against still invisible ridge

two sparrows landing on feeder beside redwood fence

left side more as you look between space in picture

thinking words and names refer to what we call this

what present in such a way those things that appear

say the word names the times otherwise what remains

gray whiteness of fog still against invisible ridge

sound of waves breaking on sand across from channel

10.23

cloudless blue white sky above still shadowed ridge

two sparrows landing on edge of fence beside feeder

direction outside of the light space made to vanish

moment of change the left side three of four follow

one making last preparations somewhere east of here

another who has just returned never quite returning

whiteness of sun in pale blue sky across from ridge

white lines of waves breaking into mouth of channel

10.24

light coming into fog against still invisible ridge

shadowed towhee landing on feeder across from fence

gradual approach to painting attraction to position

two sometimes related to one another seeing present

first crow standing on tallest echium stalk calling

second flapping to the right toward shadowed branch

gray whiteness of fog against top of shadowed ridge

line of pelicans gliding to the left across channel

10.25

gray whiteness of clouds above shadowed green ridge

white-crowned sparrow perched on fence above feeder

observed a day or so later several days after which

past the waves ready for the sky's weather a moment

position which will understand a moment can be more

instead the absence knowing that which has occurred

gray white clouds beside shadowed shoulder of ridge

white line of wave breaking on sand next to channel

10.26

white edge of sun in branches to the right of ridge

blue jay slanting from rose bush to corner of fence

moment having been for twenty years probable change

as first letter makes clear person drawn that month

thinking most of first beginning also can be chosen

unfold here the question likewise position of which

white circle of sun in bright blue sky beside ridge

windblown white wave breaking into mouth of channel

10.27

first light coming into sky above still black ridge

brightness of planet to the left of bamboo branches

lights in picture above made of clouds and branches

thinking open to this in addition to more than once

sparrow slanting across bricks disappears into rose

branches motionless clouds above sunlit green ridge

blinding white circle of sun coming up beside ridge

sunlit blue green wave breaking in mouth of channel

10.28

light coming into sky above shadowed plane of ridge

sparrows pecking up seeds from bricks beside feeder

variable continuum of physical dimension from space

motion of point maintained when body is not changed

pair of walnut trees branches slanting to the right

toward patches of light in sky morning a moment ago

yellow red orange edge of sun rising above of ridge

line of 12 pelicans gliding toward mouth of channel

10.29

first light in sky above still black plane of ridge

planet to the left of shadowed branches above fence

further likely during the winter abetted by contact

seeing remained central to light in the late spring

looking almost full white circle of the moon beside

green bamboo leaves on branches across unseen fence

yellow orange edge of sun next to shoulder of ridge

diagonal white line of wave breaking across channel

10.30

gray whiteness of fog against still invisible ridge

sparrow slanting to the right toward shadowed fence

letter given place of plants changed point of touch

covers flow to the sky taking a moment sets it free

sun disappears in ocean when along the horizon fall

shows it once a hundred times enough so I could see

blinding whiteness of sun next to fog against ridge

line of pelicans flapping toward motionless channel

10.31

gray whiteness of fog against still invisible ridge

sparrow pecking up seeds on wood chips below feeder

what might in reply to such a notion still possible

attention to given relation between the two see now

conceal the same given fact that words are speaking

what is thought better understood than it first was

blinding white circle of sun above fog beside ridge

line of pelicans gliding to the left toward channel

11.1

cloudless blue white sky above still shadowed ridge

silhouette of sparrow on redwood fence above feeder

clouds by means of which the whole point was to see

name the relation between appearance and reflection

the way a pair of birds disappearing into the light

reflected off motionless channel left edge of frame

sun rising into line of clouds by shoulder of ridge

pelican gliding to the left toward mouth of channel

11.2

light coming into cloudless blue white sky by ridge

two towhees pecking up seeds on bricks below feeder

made of four differs from three number of relations

body in words when motion is given physical example

edge of motion sight of sun mentioned previous hour

say that this can be so close eyes of same may open

yellow orange of sun coming up in fog against ridge

line of pelicans gliding to the left toward channel

11.3

whiteness of sun in bamboo leaves across from ridge

7 sparrows lined up on edge of fence next to feeder

once remembered attention to geometry of boy's face

series of drawings once again body built of aspects

almost full white circle of the moon memory looking

green bamboo leaves on branches across unseen fence

blinding white sun to the left of shoulder of ridge

white line of wave breaking across mouth of channel

11.4

cloudless pale blue sky beside still shadowed ridge

2 white-crowned sparrows standing on shadowed fence

work made on the same paper observed in early story

once more at the same time come from shore to shore

sun behind lines of reddish orange clouds reflected

channel in left edge of picture's peripheral vision

blinding white sun in sky next to shoulder of ridge

line of 6 pelicans flapping toward mouth of channel

11.5

cloudless blue white sky above shadowed green ridge

sparrows pecking up seeds from bricks below feeder

say there are degrees of less is not thought at all

person having been included some of the second half

possibility of something part of speech called noun

what thought meant by question thinking has its say

blinding white sun across from still shadowed ridge

white lines of waves breaking into mouth of channel

11.6

cloud moving across pale blue white sky above ridge

7 sparrows lined up on edge of fence next to feeder

proximity of the middle distance trees to the right

called forward to experience named the word follows

whether something else is meant whether one appears

what the saying asking is before some sort of stand

sun rising into cloud across from shoulder of ridge

whiteness of wave breaking across windblown channel

11.7

sun comes up in windblown bamboo leaves above fence

barrels on sunlit left edge of bricks in foreground

specified system of formations may be space or time

potential not referred to until divided into points

find plan for present note standing before the door

sketch point for point consequences about to appear

blinding white sun in bright blue sky next to ridge

white lines of waves breaking into mouth of channel

11.8

sun rising into windblown bamboo leaves above fence

sparrows pecking up seeds from bricks beside feeder

again only discovered limited since then by illness

again after pause the body simultaneity of painting

sees as well as remains here before which concealed

what appears what does not abyss that gapes between

blinding white of sun above cloud across from ridge

whiteness of wave breaking across windblown channel

11.9

sun rising behind green bamboo leaves next to fence

shadowed towhee slanting to the right toward feeder

change drawn on paper letter just finished pictures

so many ways lead from square to passage from field

following addition the other follows against itself

moving the center to the last sentence means to say

blinding white circle of sun next to shadowed ridge

white line of wave breaking across mouth of channel

11.10

sun rising into shadowed bamboo leaves across fence

sparrow pecking up seeds in wood chips below feeder

particular thing in a moment of time concrete event

nineteenth also refers to third appeared in October

since then the place still there meant to go beyond

moves back to the center now saying imagined things

white circle of sun in bright blue sky beside ridge

line of pelicans gliding to the left toward channel

11.11

light gray white cloud against shadowed green ridge

white-crowned sparrow landing on feeder below fence

count nine or ten leaves half point on the far hill

time lets everything emerge again what has appeared

interaction of these two roses shadowed white petal

against light gray sky red edges of others below it

white circle of sun coming up in clouds above ridge

shadowed gray lines of swells moving toward channel

11.12

sun rising into windblown bamboo leaves above fence

sparrow pecking up seeds from bricks next to feeder

relation to sixteen second form according to scheme

meaning by way of another action between given here

less the fact between concrete thing in first place

note to speak of contrast everything merely nothing

blinding whiteness of sun next to shoulder of ridge

diagonal white line of wave breaking across channel

11.13

gray whiteness of clouds above still shadowed ridge

sparrow gliding to the left from fence to rose bush

anything in order once again goes under the name of

figure isolation afloat on ground subject visualize

to hear saying learn to listen to the thinking word

entering those moments which gesture to one another

yellow orange edge of cloud above shoulder of ridge

white line of wave breaking on sand next to channel

11.14

horizontal white cloud in pale blue sky above ridge

towhee standing on bricks by sparrow next to feeder

one picture in front of garden eight forget-me-nots

path to road tied to distance traffic as to and fro

sunlit oval patch of lighter green on shadowed lawn

unseen branches of trees through which light passes

blinding whiteness of sun next to shoulder of ridge

white lines of waves breaking into mouth of channel

11.15

yellow orange edge of sun rising into bamboo leaves

two sparrows standing on edge of fence above feeder

give up nothing no more such everywhere and nowhere

see note to original in a sense know as can be seen

looks up at pink white rose against bright blue sky

sounds of unseen birds chirping siren across lagoon

blinding yellow white sun next to shoulder of ridge

white line of wave breaking across mouth of channel

11.16

sun coming up through windblown green bamboo leaves

white-crowned sparrow pecking up seeds below feeder

piece of ground you would have liked answer to form

open starting from the end the last means take back

photograph landscape taken from the air shows light

green field in foreground wingspan of bird overhead

blinding white edge of sun beside shoulder of ridge

line of pelicans flapping from point toward channel

11.17

light gray rain cloud against still invisible ridge

line of sparrows perched of edge of fence by feeder

ten if second follows this that with respect to two

form the action between the view going into details

material moment when elements position in stillness

simultaneous action of windblown leaves on branches

gray of rain clouds against black shoulder of ridge

whiteness of wave breaking across windblown channel

11.18

light gray whiteness of fog against invisible ridge

2 red finches perched on edge of fence above feeder

rather than having been observed not as it appeared

ground forms like this from space position aimed at

looking up at oval shape of light gray sky overhead

branches of walnut tree leaves fallen on the ground

gray whiteness of fog still against invisible ridge

line of pelicans flapping to the right toward point

11.19

diagonal pink line of cloud above still black ridge

sound of crow calling on branch in right foreground

those one finds in front of those flowers and so on

so they get to the other end keep in mind or forget

recording action moves further makes visual subject

two-dimensional surfaces into which birds disappear

horizontal lines of clouds beside shoulder of ridge

line of pelicans gliding to the left across channel

11.20

diagonal white lines of clouds above shadowed ridge

sparrow disappearing into bamboo leaves above fence

word already met a while ago in the perceived thing

person would mean being in the period letter quoted

viewer in front of a work asking whether it defines

action in the painting reflecting presence of words

sun rising into black cloud above shoulder of ridge

white edge of wave breaking across mouth of channel

11.21

bright white edges of sun rising into bamboo leaves

one then another bird landing on feeder below fence

need to stretch out sky this much in the foreground

this is the way in every case time is time in which

red-shouldered hawk screeching across pale blue sky

grass stalk waving back and forth below pine branch

blinding white circle of sun in cloud next to ridge

line of pelicans flapping from point toward channel

11.22

yellow orange of sun rising through shadowed leaves

hummingbird on telephone wire next to rose branches

those which being imaginary may be defined in a way

may refer to the view place at the head of its form

eyes crossing looking down at yellowed brown leaves

fallen on ground beside what's not seen on the left

blinding whiteness of sun next to shoulder of ridge

white edge of wave breaking into motionless channel

11.23

yellow orange of sun behind windblown bamboo leaves

shadowed towhee pecking up seeds on bricks by fence

impression in a certain color air that admits light

figure along on the beach after one is struck again

whiteness of sunlight reflection on water's surface

likewise moon whose light keeps time with the tides

blinding white sun in cloud above shoulder of ridge

white line of wave breaking across windless channel

11.24

orange edges of sun coming up through bamboo leaves

song sparrow flapping from fence to feeder below it

orange trees a picture of flowers in the foreground

on the way to the last act sound before the passage

moment of recognition between space of idea passing

back and forth here from the first to hear the word

white circle of sun rising in sky across from ridge

lines of gulls flapping from horizon toward channel

11.25

white circle of sun through windblown bamboo leaves

two towhees pecking up seeds on bricks below feeder

found in the field of actions relation to phenomena

describes in detail the step that led to see letter

what looks like actual color of sun comes up behind

sound of windblown bamboo leaves in left foreground

sun coming up into cloudless blue sky next to ridge

spray blown back above wave breaking across channel

11.26

yellow orange of sun behind windblown bamboo leaves

towhee landing on bricks below feeder next to fence

too close to that part has to do with sense of here

this or that time now point the place an appearance

curve of orange light along the water and sand line

presence of the person who sees it hears its sounds

blinding white edge of sun beside shoulder of ridge

whiteness of wave breaking across windblown channel

11.27

edge of sun in motionless bamboo leaves above fence

white-crowned sparrow pecking up seeds below feeder

subtraction corresponding to four-dimensional space

present of the field which seems to be part of view

crow disappearing across open green glass back door

below pale blue sky blue jay in window beside table

white circle of sun in bright blue sky beside ridge

line of pelicans flapping from point toward channel

11.28

yellow orange of sun comes up through bamboo leaves

four sparrows perched on redwood fence above feeder

color the point at which paint transforms into line

space within the range of figure and ground remains

black shape of crow on left edge of fence flaps off

quail walks across sunlit corner of bricks below it

blinding white sun in bright blue sky above horizon

line of pelicans flapping from channel toward point

11.29

yellow orange edge of sun next to motionless leaves

two sparrows perched on feeder below shadowed fence

three trees four clusters of shrub people won't see

whether we think visibly of the figure pushed aside

see the wind in shadows it makes moving on the gray

page on the table in the foreground hear its sounds

white circle of sun in blue white sky above horizon

line of white cloud slanting across sky above point

11.30

yellow orange sun rising in windblown bamboo leaves

four sparrows perched on edge of fence above feeder

find thought belongs to things this moment in which

see blue painting on glass extracts from sky's text

now being able to frame sunlight right side picture

whiteness of reflection on unseen motion of channel

blinding white sun in bright blue sky above horizon

white lines of waves breaking into mouth of channel

12.1

white line of fog in field in front of sunlit ridge

four sparrows perched on feeder below edge of fence

relation to the ground plane looks exactly the same

appearing at any time here not a sequence of points

deer stands in late November light under apple tree

goes back to looking for something to eat in leaves

blinding white sun beside line of fog against ridge

white line of wave breaking on sand next to channel

12.2

red orange edge of sun rising through bamboo leaves

two sparrows standing on edge of fence above feeder

three or four more parts the second of two opposite

ideas on the part or six standing for single couple

dog approaching from the right yellow line of light

low sun reflected on sand cloud slanting across sky

blinding white sun in bright blue sky above horizon

white line of wave breaking across mouth of channel

12.3

pink lines of clouds in pale blue sky next to ridge

motion of still shadowed bamboo leaves across fence

lines pointed out to be at the same time about what

one part among many more than projection of present

thinking appears as a kind of thing one relation to

word present in this object camera arresting object

red orange line of cloud in blue black sky by ridge

shadowed line of swell approaching mouth of channel

12.4

red orange edge of sun in bamboo leaves above fence

white-crowned sparrow pecking up seeds below feeder

foreground probable to know the aspect of a picture

whether presence gathers in sky a word called thing

getting dark so fast and light so early line of red

orange cloud below pale blue sky view from overlook

light pink red edge of sky beside shoulder of ridge

line of pelicans flapping from point toward channel

12.5

gray whiteness of fog against still invisible ridge

first two sparrows standing on feeder next to fence

at least a set of events over there distant present

manuscript of actual references version of evidence

thought of how one can catch so much light in sound

certain slant of sunlit and shadowed words on paper

yellow orange whiteness of sun in fog against ridge

shadowed line of swell approaching mouth of channel

12.6

light comes into fog against invisible top of ridge

first three sparrows landing on feeder beside fence

eye view level of stream flat surface feel of water

time something in its way taking them back to space

flatness of wet sand at low tide reflecting setting

sun goes down behind clouds above point that moment

shaft of light slanting down from cloud above ridge

line of pelicans flapping from point toward channel

12.7

sun coming up through windblown green bamboo leaves

first sparrow perched on feeder below edge of fence

only six the field shown four combinations of three

force relative to force made in many ways mentioned

still another comes from speaking and saying itself

later thought back to following now before all else

blinding whiteness of sun next to shoulder of ridge

spray blown back from waves breaking across channel

12.8

cloudless pale blue sky above sunlit green of ridge

sparrow landing on edge of fence across from feeder

various seems to mean thought how to select objects

emotional states problems of showing front and back

deer standing on wood chips next to bricks looks at

man behind the camera two ears listening not moving

blinding white of sun in bright blue sky on horizon

spray blowing back above wave breaking into channel

12.9

yellow orange of sun in bamboo leaves next to fence

two then three sparrows landing on feeder beside it

letters sending tree field a continuation of others

gathering describes after possibly much else beside

words make one see photo again as if for first time

picture shaped in which one doesn't hear end rhymes

blinding white circle of sun below cloud on horizon

shadowed swell lines moving toward mouth of channel

12.10

first light coming into gray blue sky next to ridge

seven sparrows lined up on fence across from feeder

either the act possible or not imposed from outside

some of these references followed by which is given

gaze drawn to all that is such as for example trees

there in other words not thought but rather in view

blinding white sun rising into clouds above horizon

lines of white waves breaking into mouth of channel

12.11

white circle of sun in clouds through bamboo leaves

first sparrow landing on edge of fence above feeder

relation between stream and lake one starts to feel

corresponds to something disappearing in view of it

view of sun above horizontal clouds taking viewer's

breath away line of light on page composed of sound

blinding white circle of sun in cloud above horizon

white line of wave breaking across mouth of channel

12.12

cloud in pale blue sky next to shadowed green ridge

sound of crow calling on branch in right foreground

order confusion from now on three-dimensional space

text included in the form on the other hand further

illusion of vertical concrete lines extended toward

horizontal lines of white water moving toward sound

gray plane of cloud against black shoulder of ridge

shadowed line of swell approaching mouth of channel

12.13

light gray rain cloud against still invisible ridge

two sparrows standing on edge of fence above feeder

more than in comparison less than it would be later

standing in spaces both present one faces the other

two figures on the steps say the form of a question

in view of what is seen from perspective of subject

gray white rain cloud still against invisible ridge

whiteness of wave breaking across windblown channel

12.14

cloudless pale blue sky beside shadowed green ridge

7 sparrows standing on edge of fence next to feeder

others made in the garden seem to have little color

besides those things before first of all then after

how first one then another sparrow perched on fence

floats down to the feeder in a moment flaps back up

blinding white of sun across from shoulder of ridge

sunlit line of swell moving toward mouth of channel

12.15

first pink edge of cloud above still shadowed ridge

black wingspan of owl gliding into right foreground

either event in relation to being by itself present

see also version of cover for the first translation

place of words in space on page does things to page

time in lines traveling forward past present future

reddish edge of cloud across from shoulder of ridge

shadowed swell lines moving toward mouth of channel

12.16

pink cloud in pale blue sky above still black ridge

blackness of bamboo leaves on branches beside fence

find a way out of hollow flowing from right to left

view ways to release letting appear and taking back

close up view of water in lagoon moving out channel

in context of its sound viewer's body submerged too

yellow orange edge of sun next to shoulder of ridge

white lines of waves breaking into mouth of channel

12.17

sun rising into windblown bamboo leaves above fence

red-shouldered hawk calling in field across from it

form of dimensional space with respect to transform

later form shows a possible view of point as action

3 leaves fallen from walnut tree into boxwood hedge

locking so green now after rain these last few days

sun coming up behind cloud beside shoulder of ridge

white line of wave breaking across mouth of channel

12.18

cloudless pale blue sky beside still shadowed ridge

8 sparrows lined up on edge of fence next to feeder

arrange objects according to person selected object

inside compressed on the right pull out to the left

picture in mind that sees by what it means to write

being inside an event not the same as looking at it

blinding white sun in cloudless blue sky on horizon

white lines of waves breaking into mouth of channel

12.19

yellow orange edge of sun rising into bamboo leaves

two sparrows standing on edge of fence above feeder

smooth paper the tree color idea of what I am doing

as place in the sense something speaking it appears

picture of what happened sees this turning the page

photographs of people standing in water as sun sets

blinding white circle of sun rising next to horizon

shadowed swell lines moving toward mouth of channel

12.20

yellow of sun rising behind windblown bamboo leaves

sound of crow calling on pine branch across from it

myself in reflection for instance second order view

these changes without notes indicate which passages

viewer who heard sound of those birds in background

sees one disappear from right to left across leaves

blinding white circle of sun rising next to horizon

shadowed line of swell approaching mouth of channel

12.21

light coming into sky above shadowed plane of ridge

three sparrows standing on feeder across from fence

flowing turn to fit feeling of picture this morning

appears in relation to disappearance called looking

walking across sand at low tide one comes upon rock

in left frame whiteness of wave rushing in on right

first red orange edge of sun coming up beside ridge

white line of wave breaking on sand next to channel

12.22

blinding yellow of sun rising through bamboo leaves

sparrows moving back and forth from fence to feeder

transform these from one to another relative number

distance as a field described by space from present

direction of diagonal white lines of light slanting

across walnut tree branch just at that exact moment

white circle of sun above horizon across from ridge

white edge of wave breaking on sand next to channel

12.23

red orange of sun rising in windblown bamboo leaves

7 sparrows lined up on edge of fence next to feeder

reference to the past thought of object in painting

one the other stares back at the spectator opposite

white clouds in the sky above the ridge in painting

like the window opposite unmade yellow and blue bed

blinding white circle of sun in cloud next to ridge

shadowed white wave breaking into windblown channel

12.24

gray whiteness of clouds above still shadowed ridge

sparrows moving back and forth from fence to feeder

letters sent tree in the grass pen and ink on paper

expression as thing it gathers sequence of thoughts

continually to think of things in order to be named

see what it is in doing so however asked about here

yellow orange line of light in clouds above horizon

white line of wave breaking on sand next to channel

12.25

pinkish red light in clouds above still black ridge

sparrows positioned on edge of fence next to feeder

more than ever heart of hearts object position here

based on source of air among others see also ground

humming vibration of whitish light next to vertical

black ridge below which viewer is lifting into blue

red yellow orange of clouds on horizon beside ridge

shadowed swell line moving toward windblown channel

12.26

motionless gray cloud against still invisible ridge

five sparrows landing of edge of fence above feeder

feeling in front of painting tends toward same size

appearing as in nature Saturn and Jupiter so remote

remembering what is meant by a band of light coming

for to carry me out the back door toward sun rising

yellow edge of sun in cloud above shoulder of ridge

white line of wave breaking across mouth of channel

12.27

white edge of gray cloud above shadowed green ridge

sparrows lined up on fence above sparrows on feeder

system coordinates direction see the way it appears

point also relative to form as more external matter

sparrow gliding down to the left next to bird house

on fence another flapping from feeder back to fence

sunlit white of cloud across from shoulder of ridge

shadowed line of swell approaching mouth of channel

12.28

lines of light blue sky in clouds across from ridge

sparrows standing on fence above sparrows on feeder

object impression overlooked reflecting many others

one could call it more abstract which of two to say

transcribes seen whose present also appears in view

thinking the part which almost seems to think of it

white circle of sun in clouds to the right of ridge

white wave breaking into windblown mouth of channel

12.29

cloudless light blue sky above still shadowed ridge

sparrows on feeder below sparrows standing on fence

watermarked letter sent to son daughter in New York

present as unknown attached from this point of view

interruption of breath being a part of what is said

silence of a moment between what words are thinking

blinding yellow light of sun rising next to horizon

shadowed swell lines moving toward mouth of channel

12.30

light blue sky above clouds against invisible ridge

two sparrows on fence above four sparrows on feeder

movement of object conditions that make one present

color in the background abstract evidence of theory

presence of red orange light on wall between window

frame shadows cast as sun comes up through branches

pale red orange of sky next to clouds against ridge

white line of wave breaking across mouth of channel

12.31

pink lines of clouds in pale blue sky next to ridge

sparrows lined up on fence above sparrows on feeder

almost exactly so the scale of figures in the scene

time understood as number frame one after the other

two views of huge white sun going down beside point

two views of moon rising above black plane of ridge

blinding white circle of sun coming up beside ridge

windblown whiteness of wave breaking across channel

1.1

diagonal line of cloud in pale blue sky above ridge

two sparrows landing on edge of fence two on feeder

the way the other hand appears the way field enters

space together with extension of reference to point

silver of planet going down in the west across mesa

waning white moon coming up above ridge opposite it

blinding circle of sun on the horizon next to ridge

white lines of waves breaking into mouth of channel

1.2

light gray rain cloud against still invisible ridge

motionless bamboo leaves across from shadowed fence

letters become figures in what known from the start

perspective fixed point of view drawn without color

action of movement from left to right birds passing

across followed by sound of windblown bamboo leaves

gray rain cloud against top of still shadowed ridge

whiteness of wave breaking across windblown channel

1.3

light gray whiteness of fog against invisible ridge

three sparrows perched on feeder four more on fence

selection of dates described in letter sent in June

gathering nature of things appear as something here

place of words in space on page does things to page

time in lines moving forward past in present future

gray whiteness of fog against still invisible ridge

white line of wave breaking on sand next to channel

1.4

light gray rain cloud still against invisible ridge

one then two sparrows landing on fence above feeder

one for the future which itself here again slipping

color of circle period today takes over the present

two pink lines of clouds in pale blue sky reflected

water moving next to jetty sound of wave on horizon

gray white rain cloud against still invisible ridge

whiteness of wave breaking across windblown channel

1.5

white edge of sun through bamboo leaves on branches

three sparrows on edge of fence four more on feeder

looks bigger than inches square compared with point

works either against or for terms take into account

arrangement of letters in words of poem on the page

shape of eight lines in what appears to be a square

bright white circle of sun beside shoulder of ridge

curve of white water breaking into mouth of channel

11.6

first light coming into clouds above shadowed ridge

one sparrow landing on fence two on feeder below it

enters the field appears in advance separate motion

forms of variant linear elements enter the equation

two pink lines of clouds in pale blue sky reflected

water moving next to jetty sound of wave in channel

red orange of cloud next to black shoulder of ridge

shadowed white line of wave breaking across channel

1.7

light gray whiteness of sky above still black ridge

sparrows pecking up seeds from bricks beside feeder

oblique image set tone for the rest return of ideas

colors suggest planes construct figures one another

silver of planet going down in the west across mesa

waning white moon coming up above ridge opposite it

gray orange of clouds across from shoulder of ridge

whiteness of waves breaking across mouth of channel

1.8

light gray rain cloud against top of shadowed ridge

motionless green bamboo leaves beside edge of fence

depiction of the place medium after period of views

stands there along the stream proves to be location

reflection of man in motion of windblown rain water

pooled on top of old wine barrel standing on bricks

light gray rain cloud still against invisible ridge

white line of wave breaking on sand next to channel

1.9

yellow orange edge of sun rising into bamboo leaves

first sparrow landing on fence three more on feeder

here again position object thought includes subject

idea of world in relation to blue translated figure

shadow of figure standing beside edge of white wave

moving across sand no sound ridge in the background

blinding whiteness of sun next to shoulder of ridge

whiteness of wave breaking against concrete seawall

1.10

first gray light in sky beside black plane of ridge

sparrow pecking up seeds from bricks next to feeder

landscape only once as far as remember each morning

everywhere as a sequence of positions less and less

lines of reflected yellow orange light disappearing

water pulling back across sand sounds in foreground

red orange edge of clouds next to shoulder of ridge

shadowed line of swell approaching mouth of channel

1.11

bright white edge of sun in windblown bamboo leaves

four sparrows flapping from edge of fence to feeder

fact of motion a field appears to be another system

direction of light translated to present it follows

brightness become an object in the sense of shining

light grounded in fact the experience first morning

white circle of sun in line of clouds above horizon

lines of white waves breaking onto concrete seawall

1.12

pink red edge of gray cloud above still black ridge

two sparrows slanting down from fence toward feeder

second years appeared up to but not including first

distinct but also one the other more than matter of

sparrow flapping through open green glass back door

wrapped up in towel at window lifted out flies away

pink red edge of gray cloud on horizon beside ridge

shadowed white swell moving toward mouth of channel

1.13

gray whiteness of clouds against top of black ridge

three sparrows on fence two on bricks beside feeder

reflected also saw the image related to thoughts on

location things in such a way that allows for space

present here the relation room which contains space

things appear as objects time on clock hand in view

gray white rain cloud against top of shadowed ridge

shadowed line of swell approaching mouth of channel

1.14

light coming into pale blue white sky next to ridge

sparrow on fence another on the bricks below feeder

reflection makes act of subject seen object thought

system of notation a kind of hand according to part

brightness become an object in the sense of shining

light grounded in fact the experience first morning

reddish orange edge of sky beside shoulder of ridge

shadowed swell lines moving toward mouth of channel

1.15

first pink light in clouds beside still black ridge

sparrows flapping down from edge of fence to feeder

looking at size of figure relation to kind of light

time of subject become a form therefore always less

pattern of shadowed wet rocks on sand in foreground

seen at eye level sunlight reflected across from it

red orange curve of clouds beside shoulder of ridge

shadowed line of swell approaching mouth of channel

1.16

edge of sun coming up into motionless bamboo leaves

two sparrows flapping from fence to feeder below it

field of form with respect to field observe at rest

sequence of form from here forward close to the sun

two figures standing on sand edge of water reflects

sun going down cloud on horizon another to the left

red orange edge of cloud across from shadowed ridge

white line of wave breaking across mouth of channel

1.17

diagonal white cloud in pale blue sky next to ridge

sparrows perched on feeder flapping up toward fence

still after a pause the next appeared again unnamed

juxtaposing look at first sight fragments structure

view of water moves to the right at edge of channel

across rocks wind sound wave breaking in foreground

yellow orange edge of sun next to shoulder of ridge

shadowed swell lines moving toward mouth of channel

1.18

white circle of sun next to windblown bamboo leaves

sparrows moving back and forth from fence to feeder

part of series possibly one of the first made early

four in such a way that space is provided for thing

bringing of things together making shining possible

position of thought that goes forward and back from

blinding white circle sun next to shoulder of ridge

white lines of waves breaking into mouth of channel

1.19

red orange yellow of sun in windblown bamboo leaves

black-capped chickadee landed on feeder below fence

reflection the same two ways of looking from object

form relative to painting background abstract sound

bring to appearance itself as look of words thought

see that thinking belongs to things already distant

blinding white sun rising next to shoulder of ridge

white curve of spray above wave breaking in channel

1.20

white circle of sun beside motionless bamboo leaves

sparrows moving from feeder to fence and back again

intensity of shaping space over the edge into trees

time of time made something thinking the appearance

view of water in motion stopped moving glacial pace

triangular whiteness lower left corner disappearing

circular yellow orange of sun beside shadowed ridge

line of white light reflected in motionless channel

1.21

diagonal line of cloud in pale blue sky above ridge

blue jay flapping toward feeder below edge of fence

observer at rest appears as if had become the field

so that distance between sun and fixed star near it

see the thought thinking feel the shoulders relaxed

expansion contraction breathing the body letting go

yellow orange circle of sun between lines of clouds

shadowed line of swell approaching mouth of channel

1.22

gray plane of clouds in blue white sky beside ridge

sound of red-shouldered hawk calling on pine branch

latest painting in another column view of the first

first sight after all volume variable in appearance

now the way the light changes where the walnut tree

branches meet pale blue moving toward sky blue view

shadowed gray clouds in sky above shoulder of ridge

sound of white wave breaking on sand beside channel

1.23

circle of sun comes up into windblown bamboo leaves

sparrows flapping from shadowed fence toward feeder

worked prior to the tree before the grass was mowed

locations allow for spaces word said by its meaning

mirror image of half circle 6 black letters on left

reversed same black letters on right reading mayhem

yellow orange circle of sun above clouds on horizon

white line of wave breaking across mouth of channel

1.24

gray whiteness of clouds above shadowed green ridge

2 sparrows on fence next to windblown bamboo leaves

thought of reflection awareness arrives at approach

sound refers to a passage of description see letter

looking up at pattern of black walnut tree branches

below light gray whiteness of sky become light blue

pale yellow edge of sky below clouds on the horizon

sound of white wave breaking on sand next to channel

1.25

white edge of sun rising in windblown bamboo leaves

sparrows lined up on fence others landing on feeder

landscape the kind of real difference between space

thinking takes into the disappearance time conceals

also at the same time turning away from one another

turning back toward what such that together remains

blinding white circle of sun in sky next to horizon

whiteness of wave breaking across windblown channel

1.26

blinding white circle of sun in green bamboo leaves

two blue jays landing on edge of fence above feeder

here in view volume of light given three dimensions

apparent nearly a second further position to follow

how at times the clouds keeping light to themselves

eyes open one quarter at a time hears birds calling

blinding white sun in cloudless blue sky on horizon

whiteness of wave breaking against concrete seawall

1.27

sun rising through rain cloud next to bamboo leaves

sparrows on fence above drops falling into birdbath

clear now in the changing tone between future shown

finite and separate figures understood to be nearly

how at times the clouds keeping light to themselves

eyes opening a quarter at a time hear birds calling

white circle of sun next to cloud across from ridge

swell line moving toward windblown mouth of channel

1.28

light gray rain cloud against still invisible ridge

some sparrows on fence others gliding toward feeder

letter also thinking again of beginning which views

things in place cleared for something made room for

eye sees sun between ridge clouds on way to horizon

water the color of cold one feels coming in from it

plane of cloud against still invisible top of ridge

whiteness of wave breaking against concrete seawall

1.29

white edge of sun rises into shadowed bamboo leaves

seven sparrows landing on fence four more on feeder

awareness of object later on one hand between which

letter now brought to attention photograph painting

open eyes sit on edge of bed take picture of window

rain wet green of field trees frame in a black wall

blinding white sun in bright blue sky next to ridge

white lines of waves breaking into mouth of channel

1.30

pink red of light in clouds above still black ridge

line of sparrows standing on fence 3 more on feeder

variations on trees may have looked across the room

appearance in itself what appeared becoming absence

slowly closing eyes attend to breathing bird sounds

crow on pine branch two sparrows on fence disappear

pink yellow edge of cloud next to shoulder of ridge

white lines of waves breaking onto concrete seawall

1.31

pinkish red edge of cloud next to still black ridge

2 sparrows falling toward feeder four more on fence

view of light first observing vanishes in the field

page from which positions line of thought its sound

slowly closing eyes attend to breathing bird sounds

crow on pine branch two sparrows on fence disappear

yellow red orange of cloud beside still black ridge

shadowed line of wave approaching windblown channel

2.1

gray whiteness of clouds above shadowed green ridge

two sparrows on edge of fence one gliding to feeder

twenty found responsible for selecting these others

appearances exact only showing backs to one another

favor one gives to the other part that one thinking

object places everything into boxes something taken

blinding white edge of sun below clouds above ridge

whiteness of wave breaking across windblown channel

2.2

pale gray white cloud against still invisible ridge

four sparrows on feeder two lifting up toward fence

for instance less just as much today turned out one

something within which something stops begins space

moment after moment wave one after the other moving

toward shore one breaking continuous present moment

sun rising behind lower edge of cloud next to ridge

shadowed line of swell approaching mouth of channel

2.3

light gray white cloud in pale blue sky above ridge

two sparrows perched on edge of fence then just one

becoming conditions possibility as a matter of fact

see now impression the same also listed under stone

come back to a feeling of the breath hear that bird

call see clear say what one sees in immediate world

blackness of cloud above red orange sky above ridge

shadowed white line of wave breaking across channel

2.4

blinding whiteness of sun rising into bamboo leaves

sparrow perched on feeder another flapping to fence

another version of same tree smaller scale at right

time of what appears how it emerges something there

silhouette of sparrow standing on edge of birdhouse

two others on feeder sunlit green tree across field

sun in cloudless pale blue sky by shoulder of ridge

white line of wave breaking on sand next to channel

2.5

whiteness of sun rising in motionless bamboo leaves

four sparrows on feeder five more standing on fence

fourth given multiplied by comparison form of field

relation to first physical field direction in space

one sitting eyes closed another walks in front door

hears other bird sounds of waves in New South Wales

blinding white circle of sun on horizon above ridge

sound of waves breaking on sand across from channel

2.6

whiteness of sun rising through green bamboo leaves

sparrows moving back and forth from feeder to fence

remain among the former by the end had begun to see

another figure a front view whether shows it or not

figure of the morning's light one finds an emerging

day something different which slowly closes evening

blinding circle of sun on horizon across from ridge

white line of light reflected in motionless channel

2.7

white circle of sun in shadowed green bamboo leaves

sparrows pecking up seeds from table next to feeder

letters see drawn to a close garden with tree shows

concept the horizon for which room is made location

view place of things lifted out against one another

following in such a way the appearance of something

blinding white sun on horizon to the right of ridge

wave breaking to the left across motionless channel

2.8

light gray whiteness of fog against invisible ridge

blue jay flapping toward seeds on table below fence

which one or the other day in light of what happens

attention to painting the same park repeat appeared

difference as light that folds names the same names

thinking in the sense of view something eye glimpse

gray whiteness of fog against still invisible ridge

shadowed line of swell approaching mouth of channel

2.9

light gray white clouds beside shadowed green ridge

3 sparrows pecking up seeds on table next to feeder

tree a little closer and so on it follows that when

present appearance see above said often and growing

name in the sense of being the object should appear

another in light of what is said gathering together

sunlit white edge of clouds below shoulder of ridge

sound of waves breaking on sand across from channel

2.10

white edge of sun rising behind green bamboo leaves

six sparrows landing on table another five on fence

imagine field at the same time three spaces present

point of view movement relative to material subject

here a sense whose light unfolds everything appears

resemblance in comparison to later apparent present

blinding circle of sun on horizon across from ridge

sound of wave breaking in nearly motionless channel

2.11

light gray whiteness of clouds above shadowed ridge

sparrows flapping from fence to table beside feeder

position appeared painting all but invisible figure

depicted variables given orientation in space feels

something in foreground covered over may be what is

mentioned in fragment random things only later made

sun rising into cloud across from shoulder of ridge

sound of waves breaking on sand across from channel

2.12

sun coming up behind motionless green bamboo leaves

one sparrow on birdhouse others on feeder and table

identified by number on list corresponds to present

such a thing as spaces locations so called building

physical center of object singular thought thinking

measure what is here called present spoken reflects

blinding white sun above cloud by shoulder of ridge

shadowed swell lines approaching motionless channel

2.13

bright white sun rising into windblown green leaves

two sparrows on feeder another on table below fence

see next section as soon as it changes appear above

effect on this scale measures most other landscapes

early morning line of light on the field sun rising

through branches of trees traveling north this time

blinding white sun in cloud above shoulder of ridge

white line of wave breaking across mouth of channel

2.14

gray whiteness of clouds above shadowed green ridge

sparrow slanting down to seeds on table below fence

view in the first place world middle being possible

forget to think becoming out of darkness into light

not quite what the eye saw the same color different

how what one sees when taking the picture comes out

white edge of sun in clouds above shoulder of ridge

shadowed line of swell approaching mouth of channel

2.15

light gray whiteness of fog against invisible ridge

motionless green bamboo leaves beside edge of fence

present space of the body between sections of shade

action of other material points this system follows

what one means when one thinks whether present some

thought has to do with thinking in place of thought

gray whiteness of fog against still invisible ridge

white line of wave breaking across mouth of channel

2.16

blinding white sun in windblown green bamboo leaves

six sparrows lined up on edge of fence above feeder

still remained invisible figure first made possible

figures in leaving one of two change another aspect

motion of windblown bamboo leaves a sound of shadow

moving on paper below window as words in lines look

sun in cloud across from shadowed shoulder of ridge

white line of wave breaking across mouth of channel

2.17

white circle of sun in shadowed green bamboo leaves

sparrow flapping from fence to table and back again

reverse to see large-scale retrospect seems present

called what find out only after first given thought

angle of sun coming up in bamboo leaves above fence

sound of unseen crow calling out in left foreground

whiteness of sun in cloudless blue sky beside ridge

sound of waves breaking on sand across from channel

2.18

gray whiteness of clouds above shadowed green ridge

two sparrows landing on table another two on feeder

former from later what makes system personal forces

note in view of some of these see version following

one two three four five six seven sparrows on fence

view cloud in sky coming back to present moment now

whiteness of sun in cloud next to shoulder of ridge

sound of waves breaking on sand across from channel

2.19

light gray whiteness of fog against invisible ridge

motionless green bamboo leaves beside edge of fence

point more compact that relation of width to height

day now still say the figure will bring it to light

grasp what has been less than to experience present

say that light is nothing but rather is and will be

gray whiteness of fog against top of shadowed ridge

white line of wave breaking on sand next to channel

2.20

sun coming up through windblown green bamboo leaves

five sparrows lined up on fence four more on feeder

existence of body present everywhere less this time

bodies in such a field observation of a found place

attending to each next breath lets it be what it is

sees yellow orange glow of light behind closed eyes

blinding white sun in cloud above shoulder of ridge

whiteness of wave breaking across windblown channel

2.21

white edge of sun rising in windblown bamboo leaves

three sparrows landing on feeder four more on fence

physical relates to never in the first place second

sister as part of family likeness each of two being

something about evidence of a mark-making technique

father's work once being of no interest to daughter

blinding white sun in cloudless blue sky on horizon

white line of wave breaking on sand next to channel

2.22

horizontal white cloud in pale blue sky above ridge

two sparrows perched on fence one landing on feeder

landscape enormous at foot of the room on the floor

nature of those by which are made location for four

thought of the same when naming how temporal aspect

know that doing so how out of time physical suppose

blinding white sun in cloudless blue sky on horizon

white line of wave breaking across mouth of channel

2.23

high thin white clouds in pale blue sky above ridge

blue jay pecking up seeds from table next to feeder

makes experience a way of being in world this frame

one such addition in words preceding first movement

birds and clouds a caption for photos picture words

other lines of things taking place somewhere inside

blinding white circle of sun in cloud above horizon

line of wave breaking in windblown mouth of channel

2.24

circle of sun rising through shadowed bamboo leaves

blue jay standing on table another on edge of fence

point of saying repeated waiting at screen of trees

light of everything in time let what emerges appear

moment of thought the way observation includes body

shadow of tree's leaves on branches moving on paper

first edge of sun coming up above shoulder of ridge

shadowed line of swell approaching mouth of channel

2.25

white circle of sun coming up through bamboo leaves

three sparrows on fence blue jay on feeder below it

present portion of time in which field acts on body

points in gravitational field falling into physical

how proximity could be felt in the room that is air

ear hearing sound of words make themselves known by

blinding whiteness of sun next to cloud above ridge

sound of waves breaking on sand across from channel

2.26

sun coming up through windblown green bamboo leaves

two sparrows on fence three more on bricks below it

one to change face of part even if only a brief one

two as well as part with the other left hand figure

one day white sky framed black walls bedroom window

next the sunlit left edge of window light gray wall

blinding white sun in cloudless blue sky on horizon

edge of wave breaking onto sand across from channel

2.27

light coming into blue whiteness of sky above ridge

three sparrows landing on feeder four more on fence

view of a wall field on the second floor looked out

site in space between location and nature of things

shadows of vine on sunlit side of grape stake fence

hears the sound of waves louder than waves one sees

red orange edge of sky next to shadowed black ridge

sunlit white wave breaking across windblown channel

2.28

white circle of sun coming up through bamboo leaves

blue jay standing on fence three sparrows on feeder

point of going from one to another have the feeling

see above the following subject reference to before

light spread out across motionless surface of water

after perception of distant figures walking on sand

blinding white sun in cloudless blue sky on horizon

white line of wave breaking to the right in channel

3.1

white circle of sun in shadowed green bamboo leaves

sparrow landing on fence another on feeder below it

world of leaf looks light as early summer landscape

lets come into appearance corresponding to revealed

view of pale blue white sky in walnut tree branches

viewer vanishing into two-dimensional picture plane

blinding white sun rising next to shoulder of ridge

sound of waves breaking on sand across from channel

3.2

sun in high thin white clouds through bamboo leaves

sparrows flapping down to feeder then back to fence

changes take place the moment body result of action

exactly equivalent space makes it possible to speak

yellow red orange light comes up behind closed eyes

sees motion of body on board in white water seawall

blinding white circle of sun in clouds beside ridge

white line of wave breaking on sand next to channel

3.3

light gray whiteness of clouds above shadowed ridge

towhee pecking up seeds on bricks sparrows on fence

painting things more than they appear to casual eye

at first appeared on second sight showed a flatness

something about how the eye changes the light scene

makes water moving out the channel appear deep blue

diagonal pale blue line of sky in cloud above ridge

shadowed swell lines moving toward mouth of channel

3.4

blue edge of sky in gray white clouds next to ridge

sparrows pecking up seeds on table another on fence

form located on the floor above second floor period

space relation to buildings following another thing

first step in this way a small spot in light of sun

measure according to measure face comes to fragment

sunlit white edge of cloud beside shoulder of ridge

white line of wave breaking across mouth of channel

3.5

white circle of sun in shadowed green bamboo leaves

sparrow standing on edge of fence another on feeder

control of feeling less than two hundred yards away

divided into two sections first of which remembered

time forgetting what remains thinking what is named

saying meant in the sense of what thought otherwise

sun beside line of cloud by black shoulder of ridge

line of white wave breaking across mouth of channel

3.6

light coming into blue blackness of sky above ridge

waning white half moon next to branches above fence

opposed to landscape of trees a figure of abundance

come into the open close to that which shows itself

blue oval of light behind still closed eyes opening

a quarter at a time hear bird sounds from somewhere

pink red edge of sky beside black shoulder of ridge

shadowed line of swell approaching mouth of channel

3.7

blinding whiteness of sun in shadowed bamboo leaves

three sparrows on edge of fence four more on feeder

room to make other rooms in house in same situation

references occur in first version material extended

two middle lines of words turned back on themselves

hips below shoulders allow body to fall into itself

white circle of sun in bright blue sky beside ridge

lines of white waves breaking into mouth of channel

3.8

light gray white of sky beside shadowed green ridge

five sparrows lined up on fence four more on feeder

perspective in nature's scale dead trees clear away

there still in appearance as to place into the open

hold the breath for a few moments slowly close eyes

leaf to the left of tree above fence moving in wind

light gray rain cloud above black shoulder of ridge

shadowed line of swell approaching mouth of channel

3.9

light gray rain cloud against top of shadowed ridge

three sparrows standing on table two more on feeder

assume the body of moment given dimension of volume

velocity of falling bodies in a gravitational field

lost in thought of something one moment to the next

shadowed bird slanting from edge of fence in window

whitish edge of cloud above black shoulder of ridge

windblown white wave breaking into mouth of channel

3.10

sunlit edges of cloud in pale blue sky beside ridge

7 sparrows lined up on edge of fence next to feeder

saw more in everyday object than observer described

becomes closer still set off against receding space

closing one's eyes quiet the mind look what happens

budding pink rose next to blooming one conversation

blinding white circle of sun in cloud next to ridge

sound of waves breaking on sand across from channel

3.11

sun rising in clouds through shadowed bamboo leaves

sparrow pecking up seeds on table two more on fence

following one the letter reference to work on paper

locate in space a place between measurable distance

water in channel on left side of concrete wall sand

on right white of wave blue line of sky below cloud

dark gray rain clouds against top of shadowed ridge

shadowed swell lines moving toward mouth of channel

3.12

white circle of sun in shadowed green bamboo leaves

3 sparrows landing on table 4 more on edge of fence

only one field or other feel as if one here present

first interval between another given parts of notes

breathing in and out sound of birds half way around

world the eyes slowly opening one quarter at a time

sun in cloudless blue sky next to shoulder of ridge

white line of wave breaking on sand next to channel

3.13

gray whiteness of clouds above shadowed green ridge

sparrows flapping down from edge of fence to feeder

one seems to note minus tone of tree in the picture

appearing and letting appear stands out in the open

view of cloud in sky looking larger than foreground

another viewer who is thinking of what light can do

sunlit lower edge of cloud beside shoulder of ridge

white line of wave breaking on sand next to channel

3.14

gray whiteness of clouds above shadowed green ridge

blue jay standing on table three sparrows on feeder

four extended over shade portion form between limit

makes field a matter of this view not less physical

first view of white cloud reflected in blue channel

vertical relationship to second rocks below surface

gray whiteness of clouds by black shoulder of ridge

swell line moving across windblown mouth of channel

3.15

white edge of sun rising in windblown bamboo leaves

sparrows flapping to feeder and back again to fence

see how sense of physical element continued to call

turns out to be two features ceiling above the door

light green of leaves on branch sunny side of fence

green bud coming out tip of branch on shadowed side

bright white sun in clouds beside shoulder of ridge

whiteness of wave breaking across windblown channel

3.16

blinding circle of sun in bamboo leaves above fence

four sparrows landing on feeder eight more on table

allowed to go beyond walls to garden with old trees

distance in room made by space positions a distance

close-up view of pink white rose on left whispering

something to the pink white rose on right listening

sun rising in cloudless bright blue sky above ridge

white line of wave breaking on sand next to channel

3.17

gray whiteness of clouds above shadowed green ridge

sparrows on edge of fence flapping across to feeder

one beginning to take on shape day who has not seen

parts of event repetition occurs for the first time

opening eyes a quarter at a time returning to world

weather coming in hear birds waking up in the trees

light gray whiteness of sky above shoulder of ridge

white lines of waves breaking into mouth of channel

3.18

gray white rain cloud against top of shadowed ridge

7 sparrows standing on fence flapping down to table

trees in different pictures at the same time things

concealed what in the open reflection seems to view

view of white late afternoon cloud in pale blue sky

man in wetsuit next to seawall walking toward water

light gray rain cloud above black shoulder of ridge

whiteness of wave breaking across windblown channel

3.19

light gray whiteness of fog against invisible ridge

eight sparrows lined up on fence two more on feeder

portion of shaded thing it follows form in same way

nature of those which take place relative to system

bird flapping left to right into and out of picture

disappears above waves breaking on concrete seawall

sunlit white edge of fog against top of black ridge

white lines of waves breaking into mouth of channel

3.20

first light coming into sky above still black ridge

sound of birds chirping from branches in foreground

future idea breakup of form began to see in various

back at upper left receding perspective figure head

view of white late afternoon cloud in pale blue sky

man in wetsuit next to seawall walking toward water

shadowed line of clouds in sky by shoulder of ridge

circular orange light on horizon to the right of it

3.21

sun coming up into cloudless blue sky next to ridge

4 sparrows landing on feeder more lined up on fence

limited to the first two weeks during fourteen days

same word means an intervening space between things

slanted trunk of walnut tree green of orchid leaves

below it red petals everything going on all at once

blinding white circle of sun next to shadowed ridge

white wave breaking on sand to the right of channel

3.22

first light coming into blue black sky beside ridge

blue jay landing on table sparrows perched on fence

who sees going up make at some point its appearance

absent from parallel fifth between first and second

what has been in what's to come in its call to what

has been last stands outside the site of the moment

reddish gray edge of sky by black shoulder of ridge

shadowed blue lines of swells moving toward channel

3.23

light coming into cloudless blue sky by black ridge

sparrows lined up on edge of fence 4 more on feeder

building on hill at bottom left space of foreground

shows by means first a sequence beginning to appear

inside the feeling of cold spring wind this morning

eyes open to sunlit green bamboo leaves above fence

reddish orange edge of sky beside shoulder of ridge

shadowed swell lines moving toward mouth of channel

3.24

high thin white clouds in pale blue sky above ridge

sound of first bird chirping on fence in foreground

increment of four itself referred to condition body

form of gravitation field from standpoint of degree

going head first off front of board before hands go

up head hits sand seeing stars electric shocks body

red orange edge of sky on horizon across from ridge

shadowed line of swell approaching mouth of channel

3.25

pink red edge of cloud in pale blue sky above ridge

7 sparrows pecking up seeds on table four on feeder

beginning to call then discovered spatial construct

semblance of corner a distant doorway in foreground

yellow light defining the cracks the shape of lines

curved in opposite direction ridge beside shoreline

red orange of cloud next to black shoulder of ridge

shadowed blue lines of swells moving toward channel

3.26

cloudless pale blue sky beside black plane of ridge

seven sparrows landing on table four more on feeder

during a number period lines covering most of sheet

distance in space now present appears some position

rain for days in western Australia attending breath

something about a separation between fence and vine

first edge of sun coming up above shoulder of ridge

windblown white wave breaking into mouth of channel

3.27

white circle of sun in shadowed green bamboo leaves

four sparrows pecking up seeds on table below fence

day to become an actual condition same side as when

see note above second seems both ends at this point

first to open in such a way as to see unfold itself

sound saying to listen thought that thinking thinks

sun rising in cloudless bright blue sky above ridge

white line of wave breaking on sand next to channel

3.28

light gray whiteness of fog against invisible ridge

sparrows lined up on edge of fence others on feeder

space between movement and trees continues the body

something thought of ground in relation to thinking

shadows of sunlit green of leaves against weathered

wood of grape stake fence the edge of pale blue sky

gray whiteness of fog against still invisible ridge

white line of wave breaking on sand next to channel

3.29

first light coming into sky above still black ridge

white circle of moon beside branches across from it

instant condition of time the body as material part

notes velocity of light in same gravitational field

measure the attempt to bring the word into relation

scale itself light in the expanse of its appearance

reddish orange edge of sky beside shoulder of ridge

shadowed line of swell approaching mouth of channel

3.30

cloudless blue white sky above black plane of ridge

first two sparrows perched on feeder three on fence

subject found which other one meant a sense of form

before its appearance in foreground distant element

sparrows moving back and forth from fence to feeder

to fence again cold spring wind sound in foreground

edge of sun coming up above black shoulder of ridge

shadowed white line of wave breaking across channel

3.31

light coming into blue blackness of sky above ridge

waning white moon beside rose branch across from it

rhythmic pen and ink garden such as trees in corner

replaced by what is more dimension height and depth

relation of one to think of here question of saying

one stands in a clearing as rock or tree looks into

blue blackness of sky above black shoulder of ridge

bright whiteness of moon above point across from it

4.1

light coming into blue whiteness of sky above ridge

sparrows flapping from edge of fence down to feeder

feel something space begins field is seen to appear

note the following year to speak of paint and color

moving toward sunlit greens behind eyes slowly open

sees motion of windblown shadows of leaves on table

yellow orange edge of sky next to shoulder of ridge

waning white moon in cloudless blue sky above point

4.2

yellow red orange edge of pale blue sky above ridge

7 sparrows pecking up seeds on table next to feeder

picture of moment before return to point here place

concept with a view there first think of conditions

one's shadow cast by waning white moon running down

pre-dawn sand in left foreground no one else around

yellow white edge of sky by black shoulder of ridge

white half circle of moon above fog bank on horizon

4.3

gray whiteness of clouds above shadowed green ridge

five sparrows lined up on fence four more on feeder

physical variant given time direction of line there

body of energy equal to light corresponding to hand

two legs in one's shadow against white edge of wave

sand in left foreground top of head lost in a cloud

gray whiteness of sky above black shoulder of ridge

white line of wave breaking on sand next to channel

4.4

blue light coming into sky beside still black ridge

motionless black bamboo leaves across edge of fence

balance in position pictures subject matter in room

back that runs to shoulder between door and ceiling

light coming into vertical panes of casement window

moment in room view from unmade yellow and blue bed

gray whiteness of sky above black shoulder of ridge

sound of white wave breaking on sand beside channel

4.5

light gray whiteness of sky by shadowed green ridge

4 sparrows perched on feeder 6 more on top of table

tree covered in terms of medium garden at same time

abstract from space dimension room made by distance

motion of blue black water stopped next to concrete

top of the sunlit seawall viewer looking down at it

gray whiteness of sky above black shoulder of ridge

white line of wave breaking across mouth of channel

4.6

gray whiteness of clouds above still shadowed ridge

seven sparrows on table seven more on edge of fence

something felt from the horizon coming to situation

color more of the time abstract paint also material

luminous pastel blues and greens roots and branches

floating on page no lines the opposite of black pen

light gray whiteness of clouds against top of ridge

shadowed line of swell approaching mouth of channel

4.7

whiteness of sun behind clouds above shadowed ridge

five sparrows landing on table three more on feeder

place that the moment above can show which occurred

opens into the vastness of thought without stopping

one who looks into the light standing in such a way

corresponding to thought in saying at the same time

blinding white sun in cloud above shoulder of ridge

sunlit lines of swells approaching mouth of channel

4.8

blinding white circle of sun by cloud next to ridge

seven sparrows standing on table two more on feeder

measure by seconds which at the same place relative

body in same field contained merged in its old form

physical sense of a view itself approaching present

comes at once another name spoken of that in saying

sun in cloudless blue sky next to shoulder of ridge

sunlit line of swell moving toward mouth of channel

4.9

sun rising into high thin white clouds beside ridge

two sparrows standing on edge of fence above feeder

call referred to physical position return to others

comes to each other door with ceiling's perspective

light green buds coming out on shadowed tip of vine

against weathered gray slats in a grape stake fence

blinding whiteness of sun next to shoulder of ridge

shadowed line of swell moving into mouth of channel

4.10

sun rising behind diagonal white cloud beside ridge

sparrows lined up on edge of fence 2 more on feeder

flowerings early paint on paper water color assumed

present more than space can be room for possibility

noon wind blowing through bamboo leaves above fence

window an hour later daylight savings time here now

blinding whiteness of sun next to shoulder of ridge

sunlit reflection of swell line in mouth of channel

4.11

diagonal line of white cloud next to shadowed ridge

sparrow landing on fence 2 others on table below it

when the object between sections observe experience

concept of colors sounds and numbers found on paper

what one sees changing perception of sound it makes

motionless white line of light reflected in channel

high thin white clouds in pale blue sky above ridge

shadowed white line of wave breaking across channel

4.12

light gray whiteness of fog against invisible ridge

sound of bird chirping on branch in left foreground

wordlessly the moment terms put to form of position

where every so loses itself rather open place where

where an invisible wind moves through bamboo leaves

sound on screen speaking of plants in another space

gray whiteness of fog against top of shadowed ridge

white line of wave breaking on sand next to channel

4.13

white circle of sun in bright blue sky beside ridge

three sparrows landing on table four more on feeder

place of the material part motion compared to light

weight of a body depends on measurement of distance

view looking across at green motion leaves on trees

followed by line between horizontal field and ridge

blinding white sun in sky next to shoulder of ridge

shaft of sunlight slanting down to mouth of channel

4.14

white circle of sun rising into cloud next to ridge

7 sparrows pecking up seeds on table next to feeder

return to calling on the other hand physical object

observes space to the right different other picture

one bird standing on edge of shadowed redwood fence

another flies off toward trees at far edge of field

blinding white sun in cloud above shoulder of ridge

shadowed white line of wave breaking across channel

4.15

shadowed gray clouds in pale blue sky next to ridge

silhouette of sparrow on edge of fence beside table

opaque paint left over from colors the ones we find

construction of numbers may be called space as such

lines beginning to cancel one another edge of light

next to shadow slanting across window next to table

sunlit white clouds in sky beside shoulder of ridge

white line of wave breaking on sand next to channel

4.16

sun rising behind clouds above still shadowed ridge

five sparrows landing on table three more on feeder

perception of each one at any single moment present

note relation between materials further observation

breathing eyes closing feeling inner sphere of body

ongoing sounds a bird chirps waves breaking on sand

sun coming up behind clouds above shoulder of ridge

whiteness of sunlight reflected in mouth of channel

4.17

sun coming up behind gray white cloud next to ridge

4 sparrows on edge of fence 3 more landing on table

motion in a silence about to be pronounced hears it

still plays out here an occasion in the first place

gray scale of sky from here to there and back again

birds slanting across green field ridge in distance

blinding white sun in cloud above shoulder of ridge

sunlit white waves breaking across mouth of channel

4.18

first light coming into sky above still black ridge

faint white planet next to motionless bamboo leaves

see the design as four dimensions ordinary notation

two systems each greater than small comparison with

one calling named the way of hearing in relation to

sense the same in each case different here in which

light coming into sky above black shoulder of ridge

white line of wave breaking across mouth of channel

4.19

light gray fog against edge of shadowed green ridge

sparrow standing on edge of fence blue jay on table

presence of atmosphere here by chance made aware of

blue set off with yellow astonishing internal black

red orange of chimney on left side of a peaked roof

green of leaves and rose bush in blue framed window

gray white fog against still invisible top of ridge

white wave breaking to the left in mouth of channel

4.20

sun rising into cloud above green shoulder of ridge

unseen sparrow chirping on branch another on feeder

colors same ones in painting irises garden finished

place in any location things interval in turn there

one who appears in fragments saying one whose place

opposite of thought means to gather together itself

blinding white sun in cloud above shoulder of ridge

reflection of sunlight on swell in mouth of channel

4.21

gray whiteness of fog against still invisible ridge

quail pecking up seeds on table a blue jay on fence

whether every moment of day by day of less and more

tendencies of colors in nature remain what it takes

feeling inner sphere of the body eyes opening hears

birds sees motion of wind in shadowed bamboo leaves

light gray whiteness of fog against invisible ridge

white line of wave breaking on sand next to channel

4.22

gray whiteness of fog against still invisible ridge

sparrow pecking up seeds on table blue jay on fence

about to think out of its mouth nothing will happen

first how open supposed to be second cannot be that

blue green oval of light coming through closed eyes

wind blowing across field bird calling around world

gray whiteness of fog against top of shadowed ridge

sound of white wave breaking on sand beside channel

4.23

gray whiteness of fog against top of shadowed ridge

2 sparrows next to seeds on table blue jay on fence

motion of part in three dimensions we therefore see

measured by which one place in system here compared

one counting one two three four breath going in out

car stopped on ridge road home wind blowing into it

gray whiteness of fog against still invisible ridge

white line of wave breaking on sand next to channel

4.24

gray whiteness of clouds against top of black ridge

three sparrows by seeds on table two more on feeder

possibly as early as first between home and history

black wedge a means of keeping back of figure apart

see in first saying thought in view of then appears

thinking when it speaks of what is said each person

gray white cloud against shadowed shoulder of ridge

white line of wave breaking on sand next to channel

4.25

light gray rain cloud against top of shadowed ridge

2 house sparrows standing on table another on fence

after seven one struck by fact that color mentioned

space possibility of things what they make room for

one giving attention to breath with each exhalation

5 bird calls then 4 then 3 then 2 in the background

gray rain clouds against shadowed shoulder of ridge

swell line moving toward windblown mouth of channel

4.26

blinding white sun in bright blue sky next to ridge

sparrow landing on feeder another on table below it

think the sense gives to word feel the road to town

what nature's speech repeats forms the conversation

saying the opposite of letting appear which thought

sense the present of what is once however continual

blinding white sun comes up above shoulder of ridge

sunlit reflection on swell line moving into channel

4.27

blinding white circle of sun coming up beside ridge

blue jay landing on table quail on bricks by feeder

from point of view the form gathering itself to say

name the open light shining as ones who look appear

yellow blue oval of light behind closed eyes breath

goes in goes out bird chirping jet passing overhead

sun in cloudless blue sky next to shoulder of ridge

sunlit lines of swells approaching mouth of channel

4.28

light coming into pale blue white sky next to ridge

waning white circle of moon to the left of branches

velocity of material moment above compared to light

place in the gravitational field measures direction

bird slanting up to the left body relaxing in chair

eyes opening after 10 minutes mouth begins to smile

pale blue white sky next to black shoulder of ridge

shadowed line of swell approaching mouth of channel

4.29

light gray whiteness of fog against invisible ridge

motionless green bamboo leaves beside redwood fence

photograph man combined with attitude made presence

again appears in same position what had seemed like

eyes opening a quarter at a time hears bird calling

there sees motion of wind in shadowed bamboo leaves

gray whiteness of fog against still invisible ridge

white line of wave breaking on sand next to channel

4.30

sun coming up into white lines of cloud above ridge

waning white moon beside rose branch across from it

request during same period view from bedroom window

location in space measuring distances to the ground

vertical shadow of man standing on beach sand white

diagonal lines of foam slanting toward unseen ocean

blinding white sun in cloud above shoulder of ridge

sunlit white waves breaking across mouth of channel

5.1

light coming into fog against top of shadowed ridge

motionless black bamboo leaves beside edge of fence

both described and present in one might say at most

repeats in speech painting music follows from sense

thought speaks in fragments showing far as possible

nothing made something actual thinking what is said

cloudless blue sky beside line of fog against ridge

sound of white wave breaking on sand beside channel

5.2

white circle of sun in bright blue sky beside ridge

windblown green bamboo leaves next to redwood fence

view a body say something from somewhere outside it

connection between clearing and light and appearing

yellow orange oval of light behind closed eyes hear

sound of unseen bird chirping half way around world

sun coming up into cloudless blue sky next to ridge

reflection of sunlight on wave in windblown channel

5.3

first white edge of sun coming up above black ridge

sound of unknown bird chirps on branch across field

velocity increases more than line approaching light

systems connected to the moment when it will arrive

unfolding sense of clearing sequence of which holds

one among others thinking the distance that remains

cloudless blue white sky by black shoulder of ridge

shadowed white line of wave breaking across channel

5.4

white circle of sun in bright blue sky beside ridge

blue jay in birdbath flapping up to corner of fence

fact in physical form another object moved to paint

becomes the structure flat black repeats in shadows

relaxing into exhalation waves sound breaks on sand

eyes closed sunlit green of windblown bamboo leaves

blinding white sun in sky next to shoulder of ridge

light reflected on line of wave breaking in channel

5.5

light gray whiteness of fog against invisible ridge

blue jay slanting from shadowed fence down to table

sun above the field cross hatching can also be seen

space locations facts themselves determined by body

body falls into itself eyes closing each exhalation

hears birds outside on branch half way around world

gray whiteness of fog still against invisible ridge

sound of white wave breaking on sand beside channel

5.6

light coming into fog against still invisible ridge

quail flapping up from bricks to fence above feeder

end of road taken in the form of things must change

later vision in the notes as follows abstract forms

thinking in whatever way may be yet to come whether

world shall race to prevent calamity from happening

gray whiteness of fog against top of shadowed ridge

white line of wave breaking on sand next to channel

5.7

first white edge of sun beside still shadowed ridge

blue jay on grape stake flapping toward rose branch

raises his hand looks over shoulder from background

light shines as sun between one hand shadowed other

sunlit spring green light behind closed eyes sounds

quail walking around on bricks outside kitchen door

shaft of sunlight slanting across shoulder of ridge

shadowed white line of wave breaking across channel

5.8

blinding white circle of sun coming up beside ridge

quail walking on bricks flaps up to corner of fence

velocity of material body at rest equal to its mass

axis of system relative to zero times approximation

movement of next breath follows exhalation the body

settles into a chair sound of rain pounding on roof

white edge of sun in cloudless blue sky above ridge

shadowed line of swell approaching mouth of channel

5.9

blinding white circle of sun next to shadowed ridge

blue jay flapping from edge of fence to rose branch

photograph of paintings collected forms of pictures

gap between legs spread from body continuing change

one can imagine reading as if listening to a speech

visualizing the picture or sequence of events as if

whiteness of sun in cloudless blue sky beside ridge

sunlit line of wave breaking into windblown channel

5.10

sun coming up into pale blue white sky beside ridge

two quails standing on edge of fence next to feeder

features in the garden worked from sequel to summer

space center here through which locations in things

ovals of concentric yellow green behind closed eyes

bird calling sequence of one two three liquid notes

white circle of sun next to black shoulder of ridge

sunlit reflection on swell line in mouth of channel

5.11

light gray whiteness of fog against invisible ridge

sound of bird chirping on branch in left foreground

each one distinct particular point which is present

often seems to limit oneself means at the same time

green of board black of loop shadows on white spots

water and sky don't know whether to be blue or gray

gray whiteness of fog against still invisible ridge

white line of wave breaking on sand next to channel

5.12

light gray whiteness of fog against invisible ridge

blue jay pecking up seeds from table next to feeder

place visible in speech looking back at its eye say

sun in an open clearing light only a few more steps

take breath into chest one two three letting it out

after closing the eyes feeling inner sphere of body

gray whiteness of fog against top of shadowed ridge

lines of white waves breaking into mouth of channel

5.13

light gray whiteness of fog against invisible ridge

first quail standing on edge of fence next to table

chosen the second time only different the same body

moment relative to there arriving at which is first

coming decades thirty forth learned to think summer

is to arrive at the present in and for what it says

gray whiteness still against invisible top of ridge

white lines of waves breaking into mouth of channel

5.14

gray whiteness of fog still against invisible ridge

shadowed pink white roses on fence across from gate

forms in other forms endowed with still life object

black in similar angular shards motion spiral space

see distance from pink white rose blossoms shadowed

fence next to gate angle in relation to one looking

light gray whiteness of fog against invisible ridge

sound of white waves breaking into mouth of channel

5.15

light gray whiteness of fog against invisible ridge

blue jay flapping down from fence to seeds on table

arrive outside the wall turn attention to landscape

building locations between spaces thinking of space

moment view as soon as home in part what is and not

given situation known facts corresponds to thinking

gray whiteness of fog against top of shadowed ridge

white line of wave breaking across mouth of channel

5.16

gray whiteness of fog still against invisible ridge

two sparrows pecking up seeds on table below feeder

perhaps one blind in light of ways of seeing things

abstract form today experienced something pictorial

fog against top of ridge shadowed white wave breaks

across plane of channel unseen viewer in foreground

gray whiteness of fog against top of shadowed ridge

sound of white wave breaking on sand beside channel

5.17

light gray whiteness of fog against invisible ridge

sound of bird chirping on branch in left foreground

concentrate in form things more apparent than words

sense a way that might satisfy thinking and looking

fog against top of ridge shadowed white wave breaks

across mouth of channel unseen viewer in foreground

gray white fog still against invisible top of ridge

white line of wave breaking on sand next to channel

5.18

blinding white circle of sun coming up beside ridge

house sparrow standing on table in right foreground

view of face in situation meet on sides of movement

phrase in bracket altered to read possibly abstract

resistance of fist stenciled onto tree's rings post

viewer looking down at it with eyes at back of head

shaft of sunlight slanting across shoulder of ridge

white lines of waves breaking into mouth of channel

5.19

blinding white circle of sun coming up beside ridge

quail pecking up seeds on bricks across from feeder

need to make mark repeat view of what in world word

different see when light responds to motion of part

nature becoming form opening motion of green leaves

sounds of birds on branch half way around the world

blinding edge of sun beside black shoulder of ridge

white lines of waves breaking into mouth of channel

5.20

blinding white edge of sun beside still black ridge

quail walking toward corner of fence next to feeder

there in relation to same place gravitational field

light in terms of visual look at event in landscape

diagonal whiteness of wave next to concrete seawall

slanting across moving water shadowed viewer's legs

blinding oval of sun rising above shoulder of ridge

swell line moving across windblown mouth of channel

5.21

edge of sun rising into bright blue sky above ridge

motion of windblown green bamboo leaves above fence

something less pressed by position measure of space

body becomes remembers shapes of continuous passage

body falling into itself whenever perhaps following

next breath birds calling half way around the world

blinding whiteness of sun next to shoulder of ridge

sunlit line of swell moving toward mouth of channel

5.22

light gray white fog against invisible top of ridge

crow flapping up from bricks to fence beside feeder

field and ridge in order to give an impression sent

speak of sounds on one side space on the other some

sound of birds calling from around the world return

notice the moment shadowed green leaves above fence

gray white fog against still invisible top of ridge

white edge of wave breaking on sand next to channel

5.23

white circle of sun rising beside cloud above ridge

two quails pecking up seeds on bricks beside feeder

possible in this light seeing not faced with things

double two notes sounded together almost once again

yellow at the center of purple flowers telling time

son looking unlike father in only photo seen of him

blinding white sun by cloud above shoulder of ridge

reflection of sunlight on waves breaking in channel

5.24

white edge of sun coming up above still black ridge

blue jay standing on corner of fence next to feeder

touch image at once point balance tipping landscape

morning light as bright as looking an act of seeing

see from edge of experience for half a minute sense

feeling blue green yellow light behind eyes closing

horizontal line of cloud by black shoulder of ridge

shadowed white line of wave breaking across channel

5.25

sun in diagonal white lines of clouds next to ridge

bird standing on corner of fence across from feeder

motion of material parts moment in three dimensions

place of constant zero see observation of the field

feeling breath moving hear bird chirp in background

half way around world 10 minutes from crescent head

diagonal white clouds above black shoulder of ridge

sound of white waves breaking into mouth of channel

5.26

blinding white sun in bright blue sky next to ridge

blue jay landing on edge of fence across from table

placement of system for years the measure of spaces

surrounding the fallout here appears to be a figure

shadow of man against sunlit grass next to shadowed

fence below pink white roses gate on left of street

white edge of sun in sky by black shoulder of ridge

sound of white wave breaking on sand beside channel

5.27

edge of sun coming up next to trees at top of ridge

shadowed bird slanting to the right toward branches

garden on these sheets of paper surface color again

external object over space saying name among things

light brown of windblown grasses in left foreground

behind closed eyes sound of kitchen faucet dripping

diagonal line of light against black slope of ridge

shadowed swell lines moving toward mouth of channel

5.28

light gray whiteness of fog against invisible ridge

towhee pecking up seeds on table across from feeder

these things in thoughts abstract become historical

following here again the object internal vibrations

thought coming back to the breath perhaps following

blue green yellow ovals of light behind closed eyes

gray whiteness of fog against still invisible ridge

sound of white waves breaking into mouth of channel

5.29

lighter gray line of cloud beside still black ridge

house sparrow landing on edge of fence above feeder

getting dark the trees ground as after all has been

seeing the eye reach a point light the visual world

day after day of gray fog no rain one has forgotten

sees leaves and a little green walnut tree branches

blue edges of sky in clouds above shoulder of ridge

white line of wave breaking on sand next to channel

5.30

circle of sun rising in fog against invisible ridge

sound of crow calling on branch in right foreground

motion the field before it was known moment pressed

before corresponds to gravitational mass which left

say person bone and boy two in one hand part nature

out of itself on the other becomes any given moment

blue edge of sky in cloud against shoulder of ridge

shadowed white line of wave breaking across channel

5.31

edge of sun coming up next to trees at top of ridge

sound of quail calling on bricks in left foreground

position of ordinary object hands close to painting

head preceded by ambience of shadow spaces on right

head tilts over lifts up again thoughts coming back

breathing taking in senses of sight feeling hearing

blinding white edge of sun beside shoulder of ridge

sound of waves breaking on sand across from channel

6.1

light gray whiteness of fog against invisible ridge

quail on corner of fence another on bricks below it

landscape on paper as ones built with short strokes

space on one side the other that faces being things

paddled across channel early morning cloudless blue

sky minus tide the day already warmer fog coming in

gray whiteness of fog still against invisible ridge

sound of white wave breaking on sand beside channel

6.2

light gray whiteness of fog against invisible ridge

quail landing on edge of fence above seeds on table

thought of each other in relation to there that day

two eucalyptus branches coming down last few months

more of wind this morning ridge reflected in window

two following twenty-two occurs in the next seconds

gray whiteness of fog against top of shadowed ridge

line of white wave breaking on sand next to channel

6.3

light gray whiteness of fog against invisible ridge

sound of unseen bird calling in field in foreground

things the moment turning to light at the same time

grasp the eye there attention to looking brightness

words the metronome keeping time of things going on

music playing alongside it making sound and silence

gray whiteness of fog still against invisible ridge

sound of shadowed white waves breaking into channel

6.4

sun rising into cloud against top of shadowed ridge

song sparrow calling from fence in right foreground

moment expressed in the field four-dimensional form

beginning of which is shown part following measured

crow calls three times feeling inner sphere of body

breathing other birds calling half way around world

sunlit edge of cloud next to top of invisible ridge

white line of wave breaking across mouth of channel

6.5

blinding whiteness of sun next to still black ridge

sparrow landing on table another on corner of fence

reflect position fitting sense something about show

picture at the margin spade on the left perspective

line of wave moving to the left in mouth of channel

together with the sound it makes continuous present

white circle of sun rising beside shoulder of ridge

white wave breaking to the left in mouth of channel

6.6

blinding white circle of sun coming up beside ridge

sound of crows calling back and forth in foreground

lines to bring things together show how intertwined

staying with them in present distant things in mind

fading Jupiter falling behind the earth races ahead

Venus too will soon be invisible in the sun's glare

shaft of sunlight slanting to the left across ridge

white lines of waves breaking into mouth of channel

6.7

first silver edge of sun above black plane of ridge

blue jay landing on table beside seeds below feeder

stand in possible taking of a stand outcome instant

following internal form as means of expression made

planet still up there moon higher in sky each night

visual shape of words on page acoustic shape in air

blinding white sun in bright blue sky next to ridge

white lines of waves breaking into mouth of channel

6.8

sun rising into clouds next to black plane of ridge

blue jay by seeds on table sparrow calling on fence

body in the future tense the turning light and dark

transparency of brightness a small step to the open

sunlit oval of green around blue field eyes closing

attention to breath from background into foreground

sun rising into cloud above black shoulder of ridge

white lines of waves breaking into mouth of channel

6.9

blinding edge of sun beside tree-lined top of ridge

hummingbird lands on bamboo branch sparrow on fence

active fact between mass at rest and rest expressed

where the body lowered changed raised to being done

sense of nature to the same degree dimension hidden

behind what is said to listen to the unsaid silence

white circle of sun next to black shoulder of ridge

sound of unseen wave breaking into mouth of channel

6.10

first edge of sun coming up above still black ridge

two sparrows on corner of fence in right foreground

something about still set the painting leans on box

depth flat the left half of the picture shows found

sound of stillness opening eyes a quarter at a time

green motion of bamboo leaves across fence grounded

blinding white circle of sun next to shadowed ridge

sound of white wave breaking on sand beside channel

6.11

sun coming up next to still shadowed plane of ridge

two sparrows on fence another beside seeds on table

garden line connect to part far removed from nature

present of distant things in thinking that location

wind comes up this morning bright blue beside cloud

how it appears when one seeing found what was there

blinding white edge of sun beside shoulder of ridge

white line of wave breaking on sand next to channel

6.12

light gray whiteness of fog against invisible ridge

blue jay moves from edge of fence to seeds on table

instant before words related to object ends in fact

may occur in the first or following say talking day

see how those long lines look looking at each other

reading across pair of facing pages as well as down

gray whiteness of fog still against invisible ridge

sound of unseen wave breaking into mouth of channel

6.13

light gray whiteness of fog against invisible ridge

sparrows chirping on fence others by seeds of table

remember the visual open and clearing at one stroke

thing that happens changes difference between color

sense of hearing the sound of birds half way around

world yellow blue ovals of light behind closed eyes

gray whiteness of fog still against invisible ridge

sound of waves breaking on sand across from channel

6.14

light gray whiteness of fog against invisible ridge

blue jay landing by seeds on table sparrow on fence

active position less than mass part as well as form

transferred from the body back to that system given

blue of sky green leaves behind closed eyes feeling

sound of breathing in and out inside sphere of body

gray whiteness of fog against still invisible ridge

sound of white wave breaking on sand beside channel

6.15

first white edge of sun comes up above top of ridge

blue jay by seeds on table sparrow on bamboo branch

darkness almost palpable hand that is only a shadow

element of flatness opposite half break up abstract

shadow of two legs below shoulder disappearing into

white line of wave breaking on sand invisible sound

white circle of sun next to black shoulder of ridge

white line of wave breaking across mouth of channel

6.16

first edge of sun rising next to clouds above ridge

sound of bird chirping on rose branch on foreground

search for sentiment of things in field feel garden

experience inside the present here thinking through

things in the sense of thinking one says ear by ear

person seeming in thought stone in a field or water

white circle of sun next to black shoulder of ridge

sound of white wave breaking on sand beside channel

6.17

blinding white circle of sun next to shadowed ridge

red-shouldered hawk calling on branch in foreground

sight but one forgets to ask possible space horizon

color of two parts both in some cases almost points

long shadow of man in yellow jacket standing on wet

beach sand next to concrete seawall water beside it

line of sunlight in cloudless blue sky beside ridge

white line of wave breaking across mouth of channel

6.18

first edge of sun rising above still shadowed ridge

bird standing on edge of fence above seeds on table

greens whites blues the more tones have been closer

visual experience the moment said focused on seeing

so much color out there blown round in so much wind

sunlit board below green leaves rocks on windowsill

white circle of sun next to black shoulder of ridge

white line of wave breaking across mouth of channel

6.19

edge of sun coming up in fog next to shadowed ridge

sound of birds calling in field in right foreground

field in terms of after some form repeated in field

increase in light still more direct apparent weight

no moon sound of fog dripping from cypress branches

figuring out what might happen tomorrow we will see

sunlit whiteness of fog above top of shadowed ridge

white line of wave breaking on sand next to channel

6.20

light gray whiteness of fog against invisible ridge

four sparrows on edge of fence two others on feeder

shadow appears to be on edge form likewise arranged

change expanded to scale front and side facing view

listening hears between two views the wind picks up

sound of light gray surface water moves out channel

gray whiteness of fog against top of shadowed ridge

sound of white wave breaking on sand beside channel

6.21

gray whiteness of fog against top of shadowed ridge

blue jay landing on table sparrow chirping on fence

copies after black and white view of interior paper

thinking of the distance to that location this here

light sea green board on left leaning against fence

different kind of day looking out window fog in sky

gray white fog against still invisible top of ridge

line of white wave breaking on sand next to channel

6.22

light gray whiteness of fog against invisible ridge

four sparrows on edge of fence another two on table

condition a social space room in relation to living

color level pointing to forget these two beyond see

letting breath be whatever it is attention to inner

sphere of body shadow of fence on light green board

gray whiteness of fog against shadowed top of ridge

line of white wave breaking on sand next to channel

6.23

sunlit white edges of cloud by still shadowed ridge

sound of crow calling on branch in right foreground

green dragged across the grass picture making clear

therefore seeing visual eye as eye beside the light

silhouette of hummingbird perched on telephone wire

slanting toward left edge of picture rose on branch

blue of sky by cloud beside black shoulder of ridge

white wave breaking to the left in mouth of channel

6.24

sunlit edge of cloud next to tree-lined green ridge

sparrow landing on white wicker chair next to table

where the physical becomes evident in place of this

spring transferred to balance the same thing repeat

awareness of breathing in car parked next to lagoon

shadowed green oval of light behind eyes closed now

horizontal edge of cloud by black shoulder of ridge

sound of white wave breaking on sand beside channel

6.25

gray whiteness of fog against top of shadowed ridge

two sparrows pecking up seeds on table below feeder

painted brown green that appears on table behind it

change to make the parts here become one of several

top of green tree branches against whiteness of fog

unseen sunlit shape of trees edge of field below it

light gray fog still against invisible top of ridge

white lines of waves breaking into mouth of channel

6.26

blinding white circle of sun in cloud next to ridge

red-shouldered hawk calling on branch in foreground

also at this time drawing in letters view of garden

location here nearer to what makes room for someone

how one who can read this hears that one can see it

recalling the sound of better days once upon a time

sunlit white clouds next to black shoulder of ridge

white wave breaking to the left in mouth of channel

6.27

first light coming into fog against invisible ridge

shape of motionless black bamboo branch above fence

horizon which is to person concerned part of object

full flowering of object at this moment color white

presence of place in space and time tomorrow always

something else horizon nearly disappearing into fog

light coming into fog against still invisible ridge

white line of light on horizon to the left of point

6.28

lighter gray edge of fog against top of black ridge

blue jay slanting toward fence above seeds on table

picture done with strokes pattern of color contrast

anything in the sense of this one visual given fact

parallel lines of gray white waves breaking on sand

picture of time passing in the time it's passing in

gray whiteness of fog against top of shadowed ridge

sound of white wave breaking on sand beside channel

6.29

white circle of sun rising into clouds beside ridge

sparrows landing next to seeds on table below fence

later see first three state of moments in the field

time of light accelerates toward system takes place

looking once at clouds against ridge one could look

again whenever looking again everything has changed

horizontal cloud against shadowed shoulder of ridge

white line of wave breaking on sand next to channel

6.30

yellow whiteness of sun in fog next to top of ridge

3 sparrows pecking up seeds from table beside fence

table seen from behind ideas proposed by tone clear

space on stage in perspective simultaneous sighting

thousands of days going by one after another as one

seeing a series of pictures all at once at a glance

blinding white sun in fog next to shoulder of ridge

shadowed line of swell approaching mouth of channel

7.1

light gray whiteness of fog against invisible ridge

bee buzzing at lavender flowers by green glass door

one of the many former colors done in diluted tones

crossing spaces as such space open by the fact that

rectangle of late afternoon light sun moving across

shadowed white wall of stairwell blue framed window

gray whiteness of fog against top of shadowed ridge

sound of white wave breaking on sand beside channel

7.2

light gray whiteness of fog against invisible ridge

sparrow landing by seeds on table another on feeder

object made an object of thought experience thought

moment filled by sound in position after it happens

another one of those moments to sit with afterimage

feeling of falling asleep reading from word to word

gray whiteness of fog against top of shadowed ridge

sound of white wave breaking on sand beside channel

7.3

light gray whiteness of fog against invisible ridge

3 sparrows on feeder another next to seeds on table

changes saying in things syllables together in line

substance visual in light seeing relation to people

12 hours of continuous focus makes for a particular

state of mind emerges meeting person for first time

gray whiteness of fog against still invisible ridge

lines of pelicans disappearing into fog above point

7.4

light gray whiteness of fog against invisible ridge

crows standing on cypress branch in left foreground

pass object rather than look modes of consciousness

minimum surrounded by expanse of extended resonance

sensing inner sphere of body eyes opening a quarter

at a time sound of rocks thrown into hole in ground

gray whiteness of fog still against invisible ridge

line of pelicans flapping to the right toward point

7.5

gray whiteness of fog against still invisible ridge

red-shouldered hawk calling on branch in foreground

picture of saying minimum likeness once and for all

something in the light seeing brings in relation to

right hand moving pencil across yellow paper a note

for you if you can use it eight lines on white page

gray whiteness of fog against still invisible ridge

shadowed swell lines moving toward mouth of channel

7.6

gray whiteness of fog against top of shadowed ridge

blue jay landing next to seeds on table below fence

moment of field presses flow of volume follows from

form relative to clock first approximation to which

parallel lines of weathered bricks in path slanting

toward back door below shadowed green boxwood hedge

light gray edge of cloud by black shoulder of ridge

wingspan of vulture gliding toward mouth of channel

7.7

white circle of sun between clouds and top of ridge

blue jay moves from edge of fence to seeds on table

returned from some seen painting certain looking at

sight of body dispersed space depends on two others

hand drawn line a circular orange flower pale green

stem next to pink white roses glass corner of table

sunlit edge of cloud beside black shoulder of ridge

line of pelicans flapping from channel toward point

7.8

light gray whiteness of fog against invisible ridge

4 sparrows on edge of fence 2 more landing on table

scenes correspond to further forms masses also seen

spaces open up into dwelling things among locations

attention to breath eyes closing edge of experience

unseen birds calling from half way around the world

gray whiteness of fog against still invisible ridge

line of white wave breaking across mouth of channel

7.9

blinding white circle of sun coming up beside ridge

bee buzzing at lavender flowers by green glass door

looks into present observation being before thought

just as sound in line differences in emotional tone

ends of breath feeling the inner sphere of the body

hear birds calling from trees half way around world

blinding white sun above shadowed shoulder of ridge

sound of white wave breaking on sand beside channel

7.10

light gray whiteness of fog against invisible ridge

bee below lavender flower on sandstone-colored wall

matter of things in form of likeness one seems such

seeing things derived from facts approaching visual

circular orange flowers appear as if out of nowhere

all on their own a glass of water on the windowsill

gray whiteness of fog against top of shadowed ridge

white line of wave breaking on sand next to channel

7.11

gray whiteness of fog against top of shadowed ridge

circular pink roses against redwood fence by feeder

notice from the field connected to relation between

time of light at time of arrival equivalent systems

foggy summer morning clearing out the window seeing

pale blue sky above light brown field in foreground

light gray white fog against invisible top of ridge

waves breaking to the right across mouth of channel

7.12

sunlit corner of fog against invisible top of ridge

shadowed lavender flowers on sandstone-colored wall

seeing set aside the reader sense part from subject

possibility of the original face subsequent aspects

circle of persons on boards in windblown blue green

sunlit mouth of channel vision of someone not there

gray whiteness of fog against top of shadowed ridge

white line of wave breaking on sand next to channel

7.13

light gray whiteness of fog against invisible ridge

house sparrow standing edge of fence next to feeder

three interior early doors painting turned to trees

space going through spaces stand in such a way that

sunlit green ovals of light behind closed eyes open

sound of small plane passing overhead birds calling

gray whiteness of fog against still invisible ridge

line of pelicans flapping to the point toward point

7.14

light gray whiteness of fog against invisible ridge

circular pink rose next to fence across from feeder

possibility of say the day present and past in part

different rhythm of the day after it flowering then

hand holds pen draws lines of flowers on white page

pink naked lady stem in glass jar orange nasturtium

gray whiteness of fog against still invisible ridge

line of wave breaking in windblown mouth of channel

7.15

light gray whiteness of fog against invisible ridge

red-shouldered hawk calling on branch in foreground

once opposed to endless one twenty thinking it over

visual sense of eye opening anything meaning to see

binocular vision of glass bowls on the table filled

with fossilized sand dollars five million years old

gray whiteness of fog still against invisible ridge

white line of wave breaking to the right in channel

7.16

light gray whiteness of fog against invisible ridge

5 sparrows on edge of fence crows flapping overhead

moment of each between these field when it is known

also holds the field described follows ray of light

allowing the body to turn toward edge of experience

followed by birds calling half way around the world

gray whiteness of fog against still invisible ridge

line of wave breaking in windblown mouth of channel

7.17

light gray whiteness of fog against invisible ridge

blue jay landing on table next to seeds below fence

subject matter could be seen eye looking for object

vision of thing appear in the same place perception

back of figure in blue jacket leaning toward figure

wading toward line of horizon between fog and water

gray whiteness of fog against top of shadowed ridge

white wave breaking into windblown mouth of channel

7.18

bright white sun in fog above top of shadowed ridge

sparrow standing on bamboo branch another on feeder

trees the first few weeks again see two weeks later

experience staying near remote locations and things

strike the light to make bright talk itself nothing

measure of thought one may see saying no such thing

blinding white circle of sun against shadowed ridge

white line of wave breaking on sand next to channel

7.19

edge of sun rising into clouds above shadowed ridge

sparrow standing on branch another on edge of fence

order of day that waits in story ends in completion

rhythm in the dissonance of something full of scent

hand with pen above black lines of page arrangement

orange nasturtiums below lavender in glass on table

white edge of sun in clouds above shoulder of ridge

line of wave breaking in windblown mouth of channel

7.20

light coming into fog against top of shadowed ridge

one then another blue jay landing by seeds on table

seems above the early twentieth period when endless

because eyes can see in a broad sense physical what

ten minutes later open eyes quarter at a time sound

birds in trees circular orange flowers green leaves

light gray fog against top of still invisible ridge

white wave breaking in otherwise motionless channel

7.21

edge of sun coming up above tree-lined top of ridge

one then two sparrows landing on fence beside table

consider position point of view facts which in part

light compared with its arrival measured by a clock

appearance in such a way that approach following it

everything more in relation to being itself thought

blinding white sun in cloud above shoulder of ridge

sound of waves breaking on sand across from channel

7.22

light coming into fog against top of shadowed ridge

two blue jays landing on fence above seeds on table

draw a room filled with light abstract construction

look at front and back view from behind before form

everything more in relation to being itself thought

image of object distant from already come too close

gray whiteness of fog against top of shadowed ridge

white line of wave breaking across mouth of channel

7.23

sunlit edge of gray white fog beside shadowed ridge

circular pink rose against fence across from feeder

first to return to works in addition to these views

go toward the door to the hall such that these here

hand draws green lines on white page of dark purple

dahlia in glass jar of water on table by windowsill

gray whiteness of fog against top of shadowed ridge

line of wave breaking in windblown mouth of channel

7.24

light coming into fog against still invisible ridge

grasses bending to the left in field as wind passes

present and past may follow from period of solitude

close for a time world of circle the note ends here

note from edge of experience attending to the inner

sphere of the body sunlit green of windblown leaves

gray whiteness of fog still against invisible ridge

line of white wave breaking to the right in channel

7.25

light gray whiteness of fog against invisible ridge

bee buzzing at lavender across from green back door

what could do and what it would world in background

encounter with things and people no matter how find

orange map of planet green seas behind eyes closing

speaking of weather fog getting ready to clear here

gray whiteness of fog against top of shadowed ridge

line of pelicans flapping from point toward channel

7.26

light gray whiteness of fog against invisible ridge

blue jay landing on edge of fence across from field

size and direction of field known only outside part

being taken as zero also holds other forms of field

wingspan of crow flapping to the left across sunlit

distant edge of field standing below plane of ridge

gray whiteness of fog against still invisible ridge

3 crows flapping to the right from channel to point

7.27

light coming into fog against still invisible ridge

sparrow on rose branch across from green glass door

hand of painter wave aside minor pictorial position

front repeated left side turning over given to know

hand draws black line circular orange edge of petal

nasturtium and lavender in a glass below windowsill

gray whiteness of fog against top of shadowed ridge

white lines of waves breaking into mouth of channel

7.28

light gray whiteness of fog against invisible ridge

sparrow landing on fence across from seeds on table

bedroom window walled field in drawn parallel lines

stand in such a way that here the room I go through

sees gray whiteness of fog beyond branches of trees

looking down hears sound of voice droning on and on

gray whiteness of fog against still invisible ridge

sound of white waves breaking into mouth of channel

7.29

light coming into fog against still invisible ridge

lavender flowers across from sandstone-colored wall

turn follows subject light given knowledge of place

unclear in the original sentence first hour sounded

coming back to the breath inner stillness rising up

sound of unseen birds calling half way around world

gray whiteness of fog against top of shadowed ridge

waves breaking to the right across mouth of channel

7.30

light coming into fog against still invisible ridge

sound of first bird chirping on branch across field

ground taken for granted something to do with forms

how to see itself in sight as visual sense of light

sunlit fog between shadowed branches of walnut tree

feeling of water walking across it low tide channel

gray whiteness of fog still against invisible ridge

white line of wave breaking to the right in channel

7.31

sunlit light gray fog against still invisible ridge

first sparrow landing on fence above seeds on table

spaces given relation see by means of closed system

first place following number light measure by clock

plane of late afternoon fog settling against sunlit

green of ridge words in relation to things in world

sunlit left corner of fog against shoulder of ridge

line of pelicans flapping from point toward channel

8.1

gray whiteness of fog against top of shadowed ridge

4 sparrows on edge of fence above blue jay on table

arrangement of objects breath the matter of content

front and back visual between right and left things

pink red Amaryllis stalks coming up early this year

dozens of unknown sunlit yellow flowers behind them

gray whiteness of fog against shadowed top of ridge

white line of wave breaking on sand next to channel

8.2

first light coming into fog above still black ridge

motionless leaves on branches next to edge of fence

landscape related to time another the last of these

leave behind senses come back to thing among things

allowing each breath to be as it is the eyes closed

circular orange flowers green of leaves above fence

light below fog on horizon beside shoulder of ridge

sound of white wave in otherwise motionless channel

8.3

light gray whiteness of fog against invisible ridge

five sparrows landing on fence above seeds on table

place in itself a certain way of being in the world

adds abstract pictures notion in mind applied sound

voice going on and on one day after day to the next

noticing things happening in the world of its words

gray whiteness of fog against top of shadowed ridge

lines of white waves breaking into mouth of channel

8.4

gray whiteness of fog against top of shadowed ridge

blue jay landing on edge of fence by seeds on table

landscape seems to sense of painting form of object

eye sees things to see in relation to visible being

following through speak of the breath other objects

sense of what appears in the relations between them

light gray fog against still invisible top of ridge

white line of wave breaking on sand next to channel

8.5

light gray whiteness of fog against invisible ridge

blue jay landing next to seeds on table below fence

field in other cases space given by relation to see

imagine place on the surface of the sun light there

eyes closed feeling inner sphere of the body seeing

windblown green bamboo leaves next to edge of fence

gray whiteness of fog against still invisible ridge

white line of wave breaking to the right in channel

8.6

gray whiteness of fog against still invisible ridge

sound of crows calling back and forth in foreground

calling here positions abstract almost looked first

hidden between now and settling further perspective

thought after thinking sense of the physical object

corresponding position of breath when light arrives

sunlit lower edges of fog against shoulder of ridge

line of pelicans flapping from point toward channel

8.7

light gray whiteness of fog against invisible ridge

five sparrows pecking up seeds on table below fence

until the end of health even this exhausting period

things occur in states possible even were not still

allowing the body to attend to breath feeling inner

sphere of sound of wind blows half way around world

gray whiteness of fog still against invisible ridge

line of pelicans flapping from channel toward point

8.8

light gray whiteness of fog against invisible ridge

first sparrow on feeder others on table below fence

starting point from where now this time the horizon

whole section which follows where nature leaves off

one two three four five six seven sparrows on fence

view cloud in sky coming back to present moment now

gray whiteness of fog against still invisible ridge

line of white wave breaking on sand next to channel

8.9

light gray whiteness of fog against invisible ridge

hummingbird next to circular orange flower by fence

form of world frame of mind face leaves behind hand

could appear in relation to the man already in view

red orange circle of light behind eyes closed smoke

gray blue whiteness of sky against tree-lined ridge

gray whiteness of fog against top of shadowed ridge

diagonal white line of wave breaking across channel

8.10

light coming into fog against still invisible ridge

sparrows by seeds on feeder others on edge of fence

see by means of closed system present spaces vanish

measure the arriving light resembling one mentioned

yellow orange oval of light behind eyes opening one

quarter at a time sparrows landing on edge of fence

gray whiteness of fog against top of shadowed ridge

white lines of waves breaking into mouth of channel

8.11

first light coming into sky above branches of trees

sound of water falling on rocks in right foreground

more immediate one closer than middle of most among

follows at this point as far as the end of see also

here the past present named may in which it unfolds

sense of unbroken duration rather the ground of now

sunlit edge of diagonal ridge against pale blue sky

sound of birds calling on branch in left foreground

8.12

light coming into sky above triangular granite peak

ridge reflected in motionless lake surface below it

green density of less is more changes ended by less

let alone stand in this relation what else clearing

grasp what has been less than to experience present

say that light is nothing but rather is and will be

first pale pink light on diagonal left edge of peak

shadowed green branches of trees in left foreground

8.13

gray whiteness of sky above edge of triangular peak

granite ridge reflected in motionless lake below it

present outside of which space limit of parentheses

difference between surface and sun corresponding to

ovals of yellow orange light blue light eyes closed

sound of first birds chirping half way around world

first light on right edge of shadowed granite ridge

sound of bird calling from rock in right foreground

8.14

first light on left edge of triangular granite peak

motion of wind on shadowed surface of lake below it

everything still the object little by little period

idea of such a subject present aspect invaded space

former from later that makes system personal shapes

not in view of some of these see following sentence

rectangular granite rock on edge of ridge below sky

no sound of wind moving on shadowed surface of lake

8.15

first gray light in sky above line of granite peaks

sound of unseen bird chirping from right foreground

these sketches trees in garden pen and ink on paper

location in space one other than thought and spoken

name and matter thinking of things since time still

object the difference between both ways of thinking

sunlit pink orange cloud above still shadowed ridge

corner of triangular granite peak reflected in lake

8.16

first gray light in sky above line of granite peaks

sound of water falling on rocks in right foreground

see by means of closed system present spaces vanish

measure the arriving light resembling one mentioned

light coming in called the first saying name spoken

unfolds in such a way that someone may be concealed

red orange circle of sun rising above distant ridge

first pink light on triangular peaks across from it

8.17

first pink light on top of shadowed triangular peak

sound of water falling on rocks in right foreground

in order to understand the paint he saw in language

settling into form awareness space inhabited by eye

say in the same way thought rather becomes thinking

talking about the view here sees appearance between

sunlit orange left edge of peak below pale blue sky

shadowed green trees on top of ridge across from it

8.18

light coming into fog against still invisible ridge

first sparrow landing on table by seeds below fence

how five and fifty related to memories subjects one

staying with things among which locations to spaces

light as it folds into the open conditioned subject

when there is talk of other things relation to self

gray whiteness of fog against top of shadowed ridge

line of wave breaking in windblown mouth of channel

8.19

first light coming into fog against invisible ridge

4 sparrows flapping up from edge of fence to branch

event transcended action at outset beyond elsewhere

both end here at this point there however all three

physical at the same time as heard in mind position

between what one hand grasps and the other thinking

gray whiteness of fog against top of shadowed ridge

white line of wave breaking across mouth of channel

8.20

light coming into fog against still invisible ridge

five sparrows landing by seeds on table below fence

a little too much green kind of skin over emptiness

light come into human eye could be what it looks at

pushed out over time in favor of everything appears

appearing see the difference between say and saying

gray whiteness of fog against top of shadowed ridge

line of wave breaking in windblown mouth of channel

8.21

light gray whiteness of fog against invisible ridge

blue jay landing on edge of fence by seeds on table

expression the moments multiplied by energy systems

somewhat red condition under which shifting measure

forearm submerged in pan of warm reddish pink water

soaking bandage birds calling half way around world

gray whiteness of fog against top of shadowed ridge

waves breaking to the right across mouth of channel

8.22

gray whiteness of fog against top of shadowed ridge

circular pink roses by left corner of redwood fence

day of objects which elapsed a year later described

inside space of present opposite the physical field

drawing out into the open drawing back in breathing

outside the inside everything subject emotion event

gray white fog still against invisible top of ridge

diagonal white line of wave breaking across channel

8.23

light coming into fog against still invisible ridge

blue jay landing by circular orange flower on fence

water inscribed the other hand trace of perspective

relation between space and space of things location

what sunlight does to water the water does to light

reflection of sound on sunlit wave approaching sand

gray whiteness of fog against top of shadowed ridge

sound of white wave breaking on sand beside channel

8.24

gray whiteness of fog against top of shadowed ridge

two towhees pecking up seeds on bricks beside fence

between these and being one or the other merge into

picture the scope of given view fragment in section

see in this saying measure deep far reaching phrase

translate view in reference to what is in it actual

gray whiteness of fog above black shoulder of ridge

wingspan of gull gliding to the left toward channel

8.25

gray blackness of fog against still invisible ridge

motionless black bamboo leaves beside edge of fence

close to much have been more pattern of light darks

as a look reveals an already open luminous clearing

weight of fog the sky describes the field view calm

clear to the ridge the window framed by black walls

gray blackness of fog against top of shadowed ridge

line of white lights on horizon across from channel

8.26

light gray whiteness of fog against invisible ridge

blue jay slanting down from fence to seeds on table

see from following present matter built up of parts

position of line whether potential any other number

awareness brought to inner sphere of body breathing

observing birds heard calling half way around world

gray whiteness of fog against shadowed top of ridge

line of pelicans flapping from point toward channel

8.27

light coming into blue whiteness of sky above ridge

line of sparrows landing on fence by seeds on table

painting of people living said a sense of isolation

present surface three dimensional blue beyond sight

unfolding talk of what was said object wall or room

attention to everything gathers turning into itself

pale gray blue of sky above black shoulder of ridge

wingspan of gull flapping from channel toward point

8.28

blinding circle of sun in pale blue sky above ridge

sparrows by seeds on table others lined up on fence

frame lines part of window situated in walled field

building a thing location allows sky arranging site

green trees intersecting a space made by the window

string keeping the two sides from blowing wide open

white circle of sun rising beside shoulder of ridge

lines of waves breaking to the right across channel

8.29

light gray whiteness of fog against invisible ridge

circular pink roses beside corner of shadowed fence

pattern in world draws look of object from the side

see also letter dated later photo between paintings

here where something ends and something else begins

wood or a stone in different ways corporeal surface

gray whiteness of fog against top of shadowed ridge

line of pelicans flapping from point toward channel

8.30

light gray whiteness of fog against invisible ridge

sound of unseen birds chirping on branches in field

damp grass in one sense pressure in fits and starts

together in the light of its transparence appearing

rather what passes over and through its going along

fragment listening to itself drawing in drawing out

gray whiteness of fog against top of shadowed ridge

sound of white wave breaking on sand beside channel

8.31

backlit white edges of clouds beside shadowed ridge

three sparrows by seeds on table four more on fence

description which corresponds to material substance

light periods per second placement lines toward red

found in such a way exactly here happens on its own

listening to the way speech points toward gathering

shaft of sunlight slanting from clouds across ridge

white lines of waves breaking into mouth of channel

9.1

light coming into gray whiteness of fog above ridge

bee buzzing beside lavender next to green back door

felt sense of picture in a box to others unobserved

picture the sleeper at the same time in other words

edge of experience sunlit green of leaves on a hill

eyes closed birds calling half way around the world

gray whiteness of fog against top of shadowed ridge

line of pelicans gliding to the left toward channel

9.2

light gray white of fog above top of shadowed ridge

lavender flowers next to open green glass back door

location specific first given flowers in foreground

things fold into spaces make room in a double sense

how you were before now hearing three bells ringing

door closing bird calling half way around the world

gray whiteness of fog against top of shadowed ridge

line of pelicans flapping from point toward channel

9.3

light coming into fog against still invisible ridge

sound of first bird calling on branch in foreground

one or the other one coming into place among others

moving between descriptions would appear to be seen

yellow orange of light in foreground sound of birds

calling from field eyes opening a quarter at a time

gray whiteness of fog still against invisible ridge

line of white boat lights on horizon across from it

9.4

light gray whiteness of fog against invisible ridge

quail landing on edge of fence above seeds on table

sense of form come across so far appearing somewhat

perception of something in light seeing and looking

drawing out into the open appears a movement toward

going in turn everywhere doing falling and reaching

gray whiteness of fog still against invisible ridge

white line of wave breaking across mouth of channel

9.5

light gray whiteness of fog against invisible ridge

10 sparrows lined up on edge of fence beside feeder

past description of matter concept of place at rest

end of spectrum order of magnitude effect of simple

how reflections of things in fragments relate to it

one remains in such a way sense gathering beyond it

gray whiteness of fog against still invisible ridge

line of pelicans gliding to the left toward channel

9.6

light coming into fog against still invisible ridge

circular orange flower below edge of shadowed fence

others speak of view leave which action left behind

diagram coincidence of figure comes to seem present

speech listening there arrive extremities of itself

points to which one it corresponds goes along often

light gray whiteness of fog against invisible ridge

white line of wave breaking into motionless channel

9.7

light gray whiteness of fog against invisible ridge

towhee beside seeds on table next to shadowed fence

irises in foreground same flowers perspective frame

location making room in the sense of together space

exhale slowly one bird calling another answers back

orange truck pulling up inside the rear view mirror

light gray whiteness of fog against invisible ridge

white line of wave breaking on sand next to channel

9.8

light coming into sky above shadowed plane of ridge

blue jay landing next to seeds on table below fence

coming to look at parts see eyes from outside other

vision of form together with pictures the landscape

report from edge of experience comes back to breath

resting the awareness follows exhalation to the end

pale blue whiteness of sky beside shoulder of ridge

line of pelicans flapping from point toward channel

9.9

light in clouds against top of still shadowed ridge

towhee standing beside seeds on table next to fence

light one senses appears pictorial language seeming

looking in this way the eye like sun radiant itself

green of trees on orange map indecipherable letters

behind closed eyes crow calling in right foreground

edge of gray white clouds against shoulder of ridge

diagonal white line of wave breaking across channel

9.10

light gray whiteness of fog against invisible ridge

three sparrows by seeds on table two more on feeder

think of matter in motion parts of dust temperature

light the number of periods time reference to clock

related to that sense of gathering turned away from

present at the same time absent need not be present

gray whiteness of fog against top of shadowed ridge

diagonal white line of wave breaking across channel

9.11

gray whiteness of fog against top of shadowed ridge

circular orange flower beside edge of redwood fence

letter known at the time movement toward more human

vision which confirms waking glance at a fixed view

green letters on a yellow field eyes closed sensing

inner sphere of body birds calling around the world

gray edge of fog against shadowed shoulder of ridge

white line of wave breaking across mouth of channel

9.12

light gray whiteness of fog against invisible ridge

blue jay landing next to seeds on table below fence

autumnal moon last week describe drawings of garden

location by the same house things in narrower sense

shadowed green edge of tree-lined ridge against fog

below it windblown brown grasses in left foreground

gray whiteness of fog against still invisible ridge

diagonal white line of wave breaking across channel

9.13

first light coming into sky above still black ridge

blue jay landing on edge of fence by seeds on table

eyes of two sorts experience other supposed view of

volume of landscape blue for example see sky's part

presence in what is present absent train of thought

there the ground at the same time fragments mention

pink red edge of sky beside black shoulder of ridge

shadowed white lines of waves breaking into channel

9.14

light coming into fog against still invisible ridge

sparrow on bricks flapping up toward seeds on table

possibility of same notes something being said here

light the eye can look for relation to speak itself

allowing breath to be as it is sound of jet passing

overhead eyes opening see blue jay landing on fence

gray whiteness of fog against top of shadowed ridge

swell line moving across windblown mouth of channel

9.15

light gray whiteness of fog against invisible ridge

two quails pecking up seeds from table beside fence

size of three-dimensional present follows from that

note the number with reference to nothing different

relationship between the difference in case nothing

found in what stands written present more than this

gray whiteness of fog against top of shadowed ridge

diagonal white lines of waves breaking into channel

9.16

gray whiteness of fog against still invisible ridge

shadowed towhee next to seeds on table beside fence

action it seems in part approaching end followed by

view released from vision simultaneities of figures

breathing in then out sound of jet passing overhead

eyes see circular orange flower above edge of fence

gray whiteness of fog against top of shadowed ridge

lines of waves breaking into windblown gray channel

9.17

gray whiteness of fog against top of shadowed ridge

two towhees flapping up from table to edge of fence

first days one made in the garden perspective frame

making such things building corresponds to location

appears not only thinking being taken this way here

moves toward place appears in that sense event less

gray whiteness of fog against top of shadowed ridge

wave breaking into windblown white mouth of channel

9.18

first light coming into fog against invisible ridge

motion of bamboo leaves by corner of shadowed fence

halfway to a possible other view of another implied

relation to text found in blue idea between aspects

feeling inner sphere of the body neck and shoulders

eyes closed looking back at vertical time which now

gray whiteness of fog against still invisible ridge

diagonal white lines of waves breaking into channel

9.19

cloudless light blue sky above still shadowed ridge

blue jay on edge of fence looking at seeds on table

landscape of the ordinary fact limited zone unfolds

essence in a way less essential look later in light

thinking appears the saying reflects one among many

however ground between what it says and in what way

blue whiteness of sky above black shoulder of ridge

white line of wave breaking to the right in channel

9.20

first light coming into sky above still black ridge

red-shouldered hawk calling on branch in foreground

given volume according to physical matter of moment

clock going at same rate on time in such a way wave

experience beyond thought a minute or so maybe eyes

closed sound of birds calling half way around world

red orange edge of sky next to still shadowed ridge

diagonal white line of wave breaking across channel

9.21

first light in cloudless gray blue sky beside ridge

blue jay landing next to seeds on table below fence

such a period of isolation became part of the world

vision waking from sleep two aspects hand elsewhere

relation to the way before it speaks out once again

listening to point based on two different fragments

reddish gray edges of sky next to shoulder of ridge

shadowed white line of wave breaking across channel

9.22

first light coming into fog against invisible ridge

motionless black bamboo branches by corner of fence

first mark connected noting letter indicates letter

space in locations found things structure of shapes

gathering dimensions reaching beyond one falls away

measure of fragments thinking what is said together

light coming into fog against still invisible ridge

sound of white wave breaking on sand beside channel

9.23

light gray whiteness of fog against invisible ridge

blue jay standing next to seeds below edge of fence

other given as possibility of what is meant by this

two sections of blue instance appeared in series of

eyes closing thinking coming back to breath hearing

sound of unseen birds calling half way around world

gray whiteness of fog against still invisible ridge

lines of white waves breaking into mouth of channel

9.24

light gray whiteness of fog against invisible ridge

motionless green bamboo leaves beside edge of fence

defined setting giving impression of elusive nature

found in nothing else only visual relation to event

looking out at bright white of morning light window

framed by black bedroom walls sense of inner vision

gray whiteness of fog against still invisible ridge

sound of white wave breaking on sand beside channel

9.25

gray whiteness of fog still against invisible ridge

quail flapping from seeds on table to edge of fence

show that leads to motion of matter extent in space

going at the same rate between such a way that time

attending to breathing going out eyes open see bird

flapping up into pale blue sky above shadowed fence

gray whiteness of fog against top of shadowed ridge

line of pelicans gliding to the left toward channel

9.26

gray light coming into fog above top of black ridge

wingspan of crow flapping to the right across field

source of plastic more than form whose voice period

vision waking from sleep two objects hand elsewhere

head neck shoulders arms hands hips legs feet light

yellow orange behind closed eyes hear birds calling

gray whiteness of fog above black shoulder of ridge

diagonal white line of wave breaking across channel

9.27

light gray whiteness of fog against invisible ridge

hummingbird by circular orange flower next to fence

drawings sent with letter the story further refined

space in locations found things structure of shapes

triangular gray green patches of lichen by shadowed

rocks next to same view taken a second or two later

gray whiteness of fog against still invisible ridge

diagonal white waves breaking into mouth of channel

9.28

blue line of sky in blackness of clouds above ridge

shadowed bamboo leaves moving next to edge of fence

experience of other on the surface position evident

see transcripts inserted at the end volume one blue

right foot inhale left foot exhale walking up trail

see green of trees below blue crow calling overhead

red orange edge of sky next to black slope of ridge

line of boat lights on horizon to the left of point

9.29

cloudless blue black sky above still shadowed ridge

two sparrows gliding to the left toward rose branch

landscapes message centered on two or three figures

event not yet limited landscape evening here itself

two deer standing there looking back at viewer here

walking across bricks looking back at them in field

red orange edge of sky by next to still black ridge

white lines of waves breaking into mouth of channel

9.30

pale blue whiteness of sky beside still black ridge

circular pink white rose against left edge of fence

dimension with respect to space variant also system

number between observation one should arrive at two

one plus one steps heading up to sunlit green trees

below windblown clouds in pale blue sky above ridge

cloudless blue of sky above black shoulder of ridge

white line of wave breaking on sand next to channel

10.1

first light coming into pale blue sky next to ridge

unseen sparrow calling from branch by edge of fence

said voice looking at all sides of second returning

thought of later pictures lost not like some things

eyes slowly closed sensing inner sphere of the body

following breath hearing sound unknown bird calling

pale red orange edge of sky above shoulder of ridge

shadowed swell lines moving toward mouth of channel

10.2

cloudless light blue sky above still shadowed ridge

two sparrows on edge of fence beside seeds on table

correspondence shows corner of wall garden entrance

spaces the nature of building put up location space

one sees moment of sunrise above blackness of ridge

pale blue gray sky reflected in birdbath next to it

yellow orange edge of sky next to shoulder of ridge

diagonal white line of wave breaking across channel

10.3

bright white stars in sky next to still black ridge

motionless black bamboo leaves above shadowed fence

from begin with to derive from experience structure

another form of blue covers first and second figure

thinking now and then against toward whether or not

connection between these two say speaks of relation

gray blackness of sky above black shoulder of ridge

sound of waves breaking on sand across from channel

10.4

light gray orange edge of sky beside shadowed ridge

sparrow by seeds on table another standing on fence

here the point set to one side an incidental moment

beginning from there the morning of landscape light

stone in the water thought to think what approaches

reveals itself on the one hand meaning on the other

gray blue whiteness of sky beside shoulder of ridge

sound of white wave breaking on sand beside channel

10.5

gray blackness of fog against still invisible ridge

motionless black bamboo branch above shadowed fence

first second with respect to system matter velocity

clocks both given to time measure which goes slowly

what about more what to think reference to fragment

more there following more taking even this one step

gray blackness of fog still against invisible ridge

white line of boat lights on horizon across from it

10.6

light coming into sky above black branches of trees

diagonal edge of ridge reflected in motionless lake

less absent from the start the same after attention

which is possible clear water with grass to look at

stone in the water thought to think what approaches

reveals itself on the one hand meaning on the other

sunlit edge of granite peak against bright blue sky

sound of bird calling on branch in right foreground

10.7

pale orange edge of sky above shadowed granite peak

sound of water falling on rocks in right foreground

break in the wall left background the same location

geometry earth and sky together building takes over

structure of another possible dimension of speaking

see letter in conversation with yellow sound shadow

diagonal edge of ridge reflected in motionless lake

sunlight on edge of peak against cloudless blue sky

10.8

sunlit lines of clouds in pale blue sky above ridge

sparrow landing beside seeds on table next to fence

structure of another possible dimension of speaking

see letter in conversation with yellow sound shadow

dimension of thinking the other structure of things

where it rises in what sense why something familiar

sun rising into cloud above black shoulder of ridge

white lines of waves breaking into mouth of channel

10.9

white circle of sun in bright blue sky beside ridge

hummingbird hovering by pink white rose above fence

side reduced to almost seeing point of someone else

what appears here makes it look that looks to light

thought tossed this way and that logic for thinking

this if one stands in observation of things matters

blinding whiteness of sun next to shoulder of ridge

white line of wave breaking across mouth of channel

10.10

horizontal line of fog against still shadowed ridge

first sparrow landing by seeds on table below fence

another person not the object subject of reflection

sound direction further out possibility of position

red-haired girl in sunlit orange shirt arms lifting

behind right foot moving forward about to kick ball

reddish orange light of sun above shoulder of ridge

line of pelicans flapping to the right toward point

10.11

edges of sun in branches of trees by shadowed ridge

sparrow standing by seeds on table another on fence

thinking nature takes more than the picture surface

seeing which looks into sense of perpetual relation

yellow orange of leaves on aspen branch eyes closed

hearing sound of water falling across granite rocks

blinding white circle of sun next to shadowed ridge

whiteness of wave breaking across windblown channel

10.12

first light coming into sky above still black ridge

windblown black bamboo leaves beside shadowed fence

zero extended over filament of thread space volumes

when compared with one same place measured by light

how thinking matters things supposing someone could

subjects corresponding to objects opposite one says

reddish orange edge of sky beside still black ridge

gray blackness of wave breaking in mouth of channel

10.13

white circle of sun rising into clouds beside ridge

two quails standing by seeds on table next to fence

after first one colors including those which appear

one of these possible to look at for an hour things

what is said in the fragment unbroken physical seen

part of fragment word that appears saying something

sun rising into cloud above black shoulder of ridge

shadowed white lines of waves breaking into channel

10.14

sun coming up behind branches of trees beside ridge

five quails pecking up seeds on table next to fence

same trees in the garden on paper in several places

measuring of the spaces in each case location found

following exhalation birds calling eyes opening see

dark green board next to lighter green one by fence

blinding whiteness of sun next to shoulder of ridge

shadowed line of swell approaching mouth of channel

10.15

cloudless bright blue sky next to still black ridge

3 sparrows landing on edge of fence 2 more on table

object as much as other object notion of atmosphere

letter in possible version suggesting hand or light

taken as instance a thing house encountered present

concept of object at the same time pronounced house

blinding white of sun above black shoulder of ridge

white line of wave breaking on sand next to channel

10.16

gray light coming into sky beside still black ridge

motionless black bamboo leaves above shadowed fence

picture of rock spread across foreground vegetation

relation to itself later today everything forgotten

related to that sense of gathering turned away from

present at the same time absent need not be present

orange line of boat lights on horizon next to point

sound of white wave breaking onto sand beside point

10.17

light gray whiteness of fog against invisible ridge

white-crowned sparrow on fence above seeds on table

volume referred to two systems also right hand side

same frequency of light the same sequence of places

thinking about person who left actions which appear

something becoming even more where and in what form

sunlit white edges of fog against shoulder of ridge

line of nine pelicans gliding across toward channel

10.18

orange edge of cloud in pale blue sky next to ridge

first sparrow landing on feeder two others on fence

colors which appeared first together maybe physical

eyes tip into horizontal plane back to surface look

days will continue to happen back and forth between

what will be and what has been related to something

sun coming up next to still black shoulder of ridge

shadowed blue lines of swells moving toward channel

10.19

first light coming into sky above still black ridge

motionless black bamboo leaves above shadowed fence

faded now a brownish green originally done in color

locations of four things in the sky nature of house

reddish yellow orange circle of light behind closed

eyes birds calling wind in branches telephone rings

diagonal pink cloud next to black shoulder of ridge

shadowed swell lines moving toward mouth of channel

10.20

light gray rain cloud against still invisible ridge

five quails pecking up seeds on table next to fence

apprehend around a kind of halo center outside self

letter included a yellow sound shown instead played

motion of shadows on table of leaves outside window

sounds of birds also chirping half way around world

gray rain cloud against invisible shoulder of ridge

whiteness of wave breaking across windblown channel

10.21

gray white rain cloud against still invisible ridge

rain drops falling on wet brick plane next to fence

frame of observation simply one plant broken branch

present subject relation to certain day will arrive

coming back to breathing sound of first bird chirps

10 minutes later opening eyes one quarter at a time

gray rain cloud against invisible shoulder of ridge

shadowed white wave breaking into windblown channel

10.22

light gray whiteness of fog against invisible ridge

two sparrows slanting toward edge of fence by table

left hand outside see energy in agreement with form

place the same as what has been said measuring time

head neck shoulders arms hands hips legs feet notes

passing moments going on in these thoughts thinking

gray whiteness of fog against top of shadowed ridge

pelicans circling across windblown mouth of channel

10.23

first gray light in clouds beside still black ridge

sparrow landing on wood chips by bricks below fence

later that year a great many differences of opinion

five fathoms search water find light invert picture

view looking down two feet in black wetsuit booties

gray green Spanish moss after paddle in the channel

sunlit edge of cloud beside black shoulder of ridge

shadowed swell lines moving toward mouth of channel

10.24

light gray rain cloud against still invisible ridge

3 sparrows pecking up seeds from table beside fence

bending middle of the field figure part of position

building presence letting dwell grounded responding

portrait of young man standing against sunlit white

dome of building becoming subject of his own shadow

gray rain cloud against invisible shoulder of ridge

whiteness of wave breaking across windblown channel

10.25

white line of light in dark gray clouds above ridge

5 sparrows pecking up seeds from table beside fence

centered around other against a background of other

say in this line of thinking emphasize yellow sound

awareness of inner sphere of body yellow blue green

oval of light behind eyes opening quarter at a time

still shadowed clouds above black shoulder of ridge

white lines of waves breaking into mouth of channel

10.26

light gray of clouds against invisible top of ridge

five sparrows on edge of fence above seeds on table

water in light landscape with plants in composition

subject in relation to limits view of the beginning

crow calling on branch outside other birds half way

around the world motion of shadowed leaves on table

sunlit white edges of cloud against invisible ridge

whiteness of wave breaking against concrete seawall

10.27

light gray whiteness of fog against invisible ridge

sound of hummingbird hovering next to purple flower

clock removed to go more slowly than measuring time

see the concept get to the matter which corresponds

breathing air in and out of the lungs the same bird

repeating the sound of the same three-note sequence

gray whiteness of fog against top of shadowed ridge

white line of wave breaking across mouth of channel

10.28

gray line of fog in field against still black ridge

eight quails pecking up seeds on table beside fence

physical look of object present in certain passages

horizon on cloud leaves over sky sense of two rooms

eyes closing hearing sound of car passing in street

returning to breath sound of plane passing overhead

reddish orange edge of sky beside shoulder of ridge

shadowed swell lines moving toward mouth of channel

10.29

reddish orange edge of cloud next to shadowed ridge

5 sparrows landing on edge of fence 4 more on table

perspective frame after visit earlier still on mind

place in turn open to design try to think of nature

sunlit wood chips in green field behind closed eyes

followed by sound of towhee chirping on rose branch

pink red horizontal cloud next to shoulder of ridge

shadowed white line of wave breaking across channel

10.30

light gray whiteness of fog against invisible ridge

four sparrows landing on table two others on feeder

other and the other each both saying the same thing

meaning each image in its placement one of a number

action of thinking with reference to something else

corresponding place before something in front of it

gray whiteness of fog against still invisible ridge

white line of wave breaking on sand next to channel

10.31

gray whiteness of fog against still invisible ridge

3 quails pecking up seeds on table 2 more on bricks

position of part in picture isolated one such place

one alone in relation to something abstract running

rain water caught in sandstone-colored pot standing

on top of still wet table gray rain clouds overhead

gray whiteness of fog still against invisible ridge

white wave breaking into windblown mouth of channel

11.1

gray whiteness of clouds against top of green ridge

5 sparrows landing on table 4 more on edge of fence

form at rest density of matter the absence of force

light in place given by relation to points in plane

what comes to presence word first thought continual

connection between things reflects folds with forms

shadowed gray cloud against black shoulder of ridge

line of 9 pelicans gliding across windblown channel

11.2

first light coming into fog against invisible ridge

motionless black bamboo leaves above shadowed fence

there in one seen present before arrival of absence

falling leaves forms of orange water in pond garden

shadowed walnut tree leaves and branches seem to be

like everything else these days including today wet

gray whiteness of fog against still invisible ridge

white line of wave breaking on sand next to channel

11.3

pale blue whiteness of sky beside still black ridge

sparrows landing on edge of fence by seeds on table

blue and black on paper tree with ivy in the garden

building which is finished as sequence possible way

yellow and red apples in bag beside day of the dead

shrine light in window dark above grape stake fence

reddish orange edge of sky beside shoulder of ridge

line of pelicans gliding to the left toward channel

11.4

light coming into clouds against top of black ridge

12 sparrows pecking up seeds on table next to fence

each in the sense of an event seen to take shape in

follows in letter above the yellow of sound in blue

words pointing toward things we don't see invisible

some country from whose shores no traveller returns

dark gray of clouds against black shoulder of ridge

white line of wave breaking on sand next to channel

11.5

pink light coming into lines of clouds beside ridge

hummingbird whirring by purple flowers above bricks

altogether out of place impression which seems more

abstract form which circulates first seeing looking

complete white light in homage to the square window

framed gray black walls painting landscape on right

yellow orange line of cloud above shoulder of ridge

shadowed swell lines moving toward mouth of channel

11.6

yellow red orange of clouds above still black ridge

7 sparrows landing on table others on edge of fence

multiply by this continuity which differs from that

distance from each other plane paper chosen so that

thinking when one says this or that thing situation

given set of events according to thinking of things

red orange edge of cloud by black shoulder of ridge

diagonal white line of wave breaking across channel

11.7

cloudless pale blue sky beside still shadowed ridge

3 sparrows next to seeds on table another on feeder

present before solitude constructs forms of subject

based on canvas sight gazed at through dimming eyes

attentive to arrival of thinking see given sequence

what is thought about appears after bends toward it

blinding white sun rising next to shoulder of ridge

white line of wave breaking across mouth of channel

11.8

pink light coming into cloud next to shadowed ridge

eight quails pecking up seeds on table beside fence

last week pen ink graphite on paper in another hand

grasp structure touch its nature location into what

attention to arrival of thinking see given sequence

what is thought about appears after bends toward it

yellow red orange of clouds above shoulder of ridge

line of pelicans flapping to the right toward point

11.9

light gray rain cloud still against invisible ridge

12 sparrows pecking up seeds on table next to fence

shape seen in anything else none which can be given

translated to letter above moved to three elsewhere

breathing in count three bees beside purple flowers

hold for six out for nine followed by bell sounding

gray rain cloud against invisible shoulder of ridge

white wave breaking into windblown mouth of channel

11.10

light coming into clouds above still shadowed ridge

sparrows flapping toward seeds on table below fence

water painting done late registers picture opposite

being movement looking holding something like light

place something in such a way standing shows itself

before that in manner with what and how it comes to

yellow circle of sun rising into clouds above ridge

shadowed line of swell approaching mouth of channel

11.11

cloudless blue white sky above still shadowed ridge

10 sparrows pecking up seeds on table next to fence

observing the first three correspond further motion

taken in direction of the plane vanishing wave line

head neck shoulders chest arms back lower legs feet

yellow behind closed eyes birds calling on branches

blinding white yellow sun next to shoulder of ridge

white lines of waves breaking into mouth of channel

11.12

cloudless pale blue sky beside still shadowed ridge

sparrows landing by seeds on table towhees on fence

physical long after all that which continues beyond

language scene of the lake close to intuitive space

attending to inner sphere of body letting breathing

be the sound of birds calling half way around world

blinding white circle of sun next to shadowed ridge

white lines of waves breaking into mouth of channel

11.13

cloudless bright blue sky beside sunlit green ridge

sparrows by seeds on table another landing on fence

collection transferred to place dated titled garden

possible to conceive of rooms made by this location

blue jay splashes in birdbath white-crowned sparrow

slanting toward fence sound of jet passing overhead

blinding white sun in sky across from edge of ridge

diagonal white line of wave breaking across channel

11.14

diagonal line of cloud in pale blue sky above ridge

sparrows and quails by seeds on table next to fence

certain story of situations periods possible moment

here the same detail see edition of sound described

after breathing in out sound of red-shouldered hawk

calling on branch other birds half way around world

blinding white sun in cloud above shoulder of ridge

sunlit line of swell moving toward mouth of channel

11.15

first pink light in clouds beside still black ridge

7 sparrows next to seeds on table another on feeder

sense of one stretched out ground down in the water

something clearing opens follows from its beginning

one remembers lemon tree on a hill behind the house

views of the mountain gone this morning French time

yellow red orange of clouds above shoulder of ridge

shadowed swell lines moving toward mouth of channel

11.16

cloudless blue white sky above still shadowed ridge

6 sparrows next to seeds on table another on feeder

density of systems based on description of physical

plane there in time of section circles round points

in such a way begin to see light of day the form of

name related to unconcealed something setting forth

sunlit edges of fog against black shoulder of ridge

line of pelicans flapping from point toward channel

11.17

first light in pale blue sky next to shadowed ridge

hummingbird stops on apple tree branch above bricks

contemplate longer real called object of appearance

orientation close to those objects resting in space

reflection circles around itself matters and things

thinking of reference to path on which step by step

yellow orange edge of sky next to shoulder of ridge

line of pelicans flapping from channel toward point

11.18

reddish edge of gray cloud beside still black ridge

sparrow landing by seeds on table two more on fence

place selected period here for the first time shows

making something appear present in this or that way

fact of the matter follows shows how and what sense

two thoughts drawn into each other one returning to

pink red edges of clouds by black shoulder of ridge

white line of wave breaking on sand next to channel

11.19

light gray whiteness of fog against invisible ridge

10 sparrows pecking up seeds on table next to fence

one moves in any direction would be possible to say

also in a color version of some taken together kind

one walking along bricks below clouds passing below

full moon above to enter the earth's shadow eclipse

gray whiteness of fog still against invisible ridge

white line of wave breaking into motionless channel

11.20

whiteness of stars in moonlit sky above black ridge

bright white circle of moon above shadowed branches

what saying goes so far light and shade time of day

open at beginning of thinking ground see reflection

feel head neck shoulders chest arms lower legs feet

will be hearing birds breathe thinking hearing bell

first light coming into sky above still black ridge

white circle of moon in blue black sky beside point

11.21

cloudless bright blue sky beside sunlit green ridge

three quails pecking up seeds on table beside fence

forms of nature spaces of reference state of motion

light at points tangent to circle deflected in path

one the white room three horizontal windows covered

blue taped plastic painted tarp over finished floor

blinding white circle of sun next to shadowed ridge

sound of waves breaking on sand across from channel

11.22

first light coming into sky above still black ridge

10 sparrows landing by seeds on table next to fence

object in the form of appearance following arriving

space now after a lapse of years made closer to say

yellow edge of light behind eyes closed opening see

apple on branch birds calling half way around world

pink yellow orange of sky next to shoulder of ridge

white line of wave breaking into motionless channel

11.23

pale blue whiteness of sky beside still black ridge

15 sparrows pecking up seeds on table next to fence

first view of the garden ivy followed to the ground

appears in time still concealed in terms of the two

attention resting on breathing eyes closing hearing

chainsaw neighbor talking bee buzzing purple flower

horizontal red orange lines of clouds next to ridge

sound of waves breaking on sand across from channel

11.24

cloudless pale blue sky beside still shadowed ridge

11 sparrows pecking up seeds on table next to fence

period of time to say event which they did not have

inscribed in a sound beyond not known what happened

thought today in relation to between now and before

hand keeping something concealed calling name sense

blinding whiteness of sun next to still black ridge

line of pelicans flapping from point toward channel

11.25

pale blue light in sky next to still shadowed ridge

sparrow pecking up seeds on table two more on fence

account of the way a particular morning detail then

beginning word open present something known blurred

also occurs when thinking of something more between

consequence of experiences related to word it names

pink lines of clouds in pale blue sky next to ridge

shadowed swell lines moving toward mouth of channel

11.26

sunlit line of cloud in pale blue sky next to ridge

12 sparrows landing by seeds on table next to fence

think of states of motion bodies in space continuum

calculate the angle toward side of increasing light

possible which stands falls walks rests unconcealed

nature given we can see relation to ground thinking

yellow orange clouds beside black shoulder of ridge

pelicans flapping from right to left toward channel

11.27

pink red edge of sky beside black branches of trees

14 sparrows pecking up seeds on table more on fence

something out of which appears touches those points

perceive the leap before seeing some time far trees

light in the way it is there the sense of dimension

something like original something on the other hand

yellow orange of sun beside black shoulder of ridge

shadowed swell lines moving toward mouth of channel

11.28

cloudless pale blue sky beside still shadowed ridge

sparrows landing on table flapping back up to fence

first to leave first here reference to similarities

late still remains building sense of letting appear

moment positions more than in relation to appearing

opened into nothing but something still approaching

yellow orange circle of sun coming up next to ridge

shadowed blue lines of swells moving toward channel

11.29

cloudless blue white sky next to sunlit green ridge

11 sparrows beside seeds on table blue jay on fence

anything part of nothing moment form of the present

certain version of sounds different remain the same

something near to another word stands for the other

connection between point and ground whether and how

blinding whiteness of sun next to shoulder of ridge

parallel blue lines of swells moving toward channel

11.30

first light coming into sky above still black ridge

curve of waning white moon beside shadowed branches

landscape simplified lights flat the picture echoes

less not open to experience light the luminous name

account of making one may see thinking if one looks

actions of thought and ground between is and can be

reddish orange edge of sky beside shoulder of ridge

sound of waves breaking on sand across from channel

12.1

reddish orange edge of sky beside shadowed branches

11 sparrows pecking up seeds from table below fence

mention in part seems physical object as from point

describe the side of light system the field of form

form becoming ordering thinking amounts to the same

once again finds itself subject terms of reflection

yellow orange whiteness of sun rising next to ridge

shadowed line of swell approaching mouth of channel

12.2

light pink lines of clouds beside shadowed branches

15 sparrows landing by seeds on table next to fence

relate to physical left out followed path described

slicing down the canvas real and rest in reflection

sunlit spider webs stretched between purple flowers

bird landing on apple tree branch beside brick path

blinding white circle of sun coming up beside ridge

white line of wave breaking on sand next to channel

12.3

light gray whiteness of fog against invisible ridge

7 sparrows pecking up seeds from table beside fence

which might possibly have been suggesting date here

something made present among the nature of building

reflection on name with two other names rocks water

emerging presence appears motion of points in space

gray whiteness of fog against top of shadowed ridge

white lines of wave breaking on sand beside channel

12.4

gray whiteness of fog against top of shadowed ridge

14 sparrows beside seeds on table blue jay on fence

there from part of its end then from least fragment

further among paper versions twelve of twenty pages

here also what appears from out of which everything

when for once to say before thinking beyond at most

light gray fog beside still black shoulder of ridge

whiteness of wave breaking against concrete seawall

12.5

light gray whiteness of fog against invisible ridge

tenth sparrow landing by seeds on table below fence

attention and state of mind see point of comparison

sense here physical thinking thought closer to what

feeling of breathing in out eyes slowly opening see

hummingbird passing purple flower beside brick path

gray whiteness of fog against still invisible ridge

white line of wave breaking on sand next to channel

12.6

light gray whiteness of fog against invisible ridge

10 sparrows pecking up seeds from table below fence

space to make both later statements physically real

light turned the side on a path gravitational field

time also thinks in a way eye toward what it can be

there being set apart from others relates to ground

gray whiteness of fog still against invisible ridge

lines of waves breaking on sand across from channel

12.7

sunlit white clouds in light blue sky next to ridge

sparrows flapping toward seeds on table below fence

follows most closely of all out of touch with ideas

horizon traced by the scene thinning lines extended

yellow oval of light behind eyes slowly opening see

hummingbird lift above purple flowers by brick path

sun rising into cloud across from shoulder of ridge

white line of wave breaking on sand next to channel

12.8

light coming into fog against top of shadowed ridge

one then two sparrows by seeds on table below fence

connection with other note mention under green nest

nature of location in space think for a while house

head neck shoulders upper arms hands legs feet hear

sound of unknown bird calling half way around world

gray whiteness of fog against top of shadowed ridge

sound of white wave breaking on sand beside channel

12.9

shadowed gray of cloud in pale blue sky above ridge

3 sparrows next to seeds on table 4 others on fence

something which can appear here a part to be played

matter inscribed for sounds to show in two versions

there being set apart from others relates to ground

sense in different way approach toward center midst

reddish orange edge of sky beside cloud above ridge

white line of wave breaking on sand next to channel

12.10

cloudless blue white sky next to sunlit green ridge

two towhees pecking up seeds on table next to fence

difference between pictures relation of hand to man

open approaching present way show what can be space

holds the center which relates to reference to name

reflection of subject thinking vision which appears

reddish orange edge of sky beside shoulder of ridge

line of pelicans flapping from point toward channel

12.11

bright white stars in blackness of sky beside ridge

black shape of motionless bamboo leaves above fence

physical effect of the point two in the first place

light passing the side of a body directed toward it

written in stars the hand that heads back toward it

less or more a form of thinking emptiness of things

orange of lights on horizon below shoulder of ridge

sound of waves breaking on sand across from channel

12.12

light gray rain cloud against still invisible ridge

sparrows and towhees by seeds on table beside fence

two bottles piece of glass objects of an apparition

hint of space in former times found rest under feet

possible sequences the physical form of the subject

what could be the third one turned toward something

gray rain clouds against shoulder of shadowed ridge

whiteness of wave breaking across windblown channel

12.13

gray black rain cloud against still invisible ridge

drops falling from motionless branches across fence

drawing of period made in garden reaction to letter

black two hundred years ago enter oneness in things

being reflection turning toward inverted upper hand

what one would otherwise call a part of the subject

gray black rain cloud still against invisible ridge

shadowed gray waves breaking into windblown channel

12.14

light coming into clouds above still shadowed ridge

sparrows landing next to seeds on table below fence

things that appear before others occurring together

later thoughts concern hills water leaves landscape

breathing in breathing out eyes slowly opening sees

red-throated hummingbird purple flower above bricks

shadowed clouds above still black shoulder of ridge

line of pelicans flapping to the right toward point

12.15

clouds in blue white sky above shadowed green ridge

sparrows beside seeds on table flapping up to fence

pictures point to things one in answer to the other

traversed dimensions a span of time close to object

object of structure at same time physical dimension

become another voice both able to speak of position

blinding whiteness of sun below cloud next to ridge

shadowed swell lines moving toward mouth of channel

12.16

white cloud in bright blue sky above shadowed ridge

16 sparrows landing by seeds on table next to fence

condition of thing part in motion relation to space

body here constant distance of light going past sun

series of moments light coming into sky followed by

two sunlit feet standing on a cold wet black street

blinding white circle of sun in cloud next to ridge

line of pelicans flapping from channel toward point

12.17

light coming into blue whiteness of sky above ridge

quails and sparrows by seeds on table next to fence

objects composed physical end to forms of awareness

bodies after ground not too far away one half water

impression after circling around how every sentence

moved beyond apparent thinking nothing else besides

yellow orange circle of sun above shoulder of ridge

white line of wave breaking on sand next to channel

                                        3.24.19 - 12.17.21

Johnny Ratcliffe

Stephen Ratcliffe's most recent books are *w i n d o w* (Spuyten Duyvil, 2024), *Black and Yellow Notebooks* (BlazeVOX [books], 2023) *Some Time / poems 1970-1980* (Spuyten Duyvil, 2022), *Barbara Guest & Stephen Ratcliffe : Letters* (Chax, 2022), and *Rocks and More Rocks* (Cuneiform, 2021). His ongoing series of eight 1,000-page books written in 1,000 consecutive days is available online at Editions Eclipse (http://eclipsearchive. org/projects/HUMAN/) and his daily poems-plus-photographs are at Temporality (stephenratcliffe. blogspot.com). Publisher of Avenue B books and Emeritus Professor at Mills College in Oakland, he has lived in Bolinas California since 1973.